Also by Frederick Leboyer

BIRTH WITHOUT VIOLENCE

INNER BEAUTY, INNER LIGHT

Loving

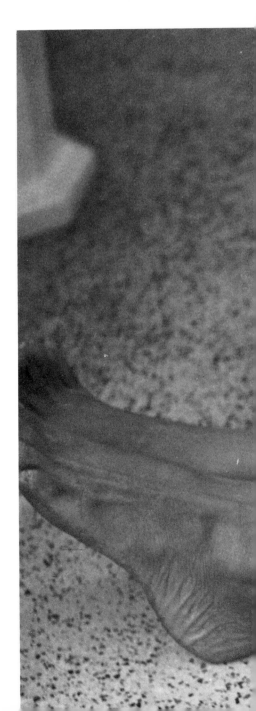

ALFRED A. KNOPF

NEW YORK

1982

Hands

by **FREDERICK LEBOYER**

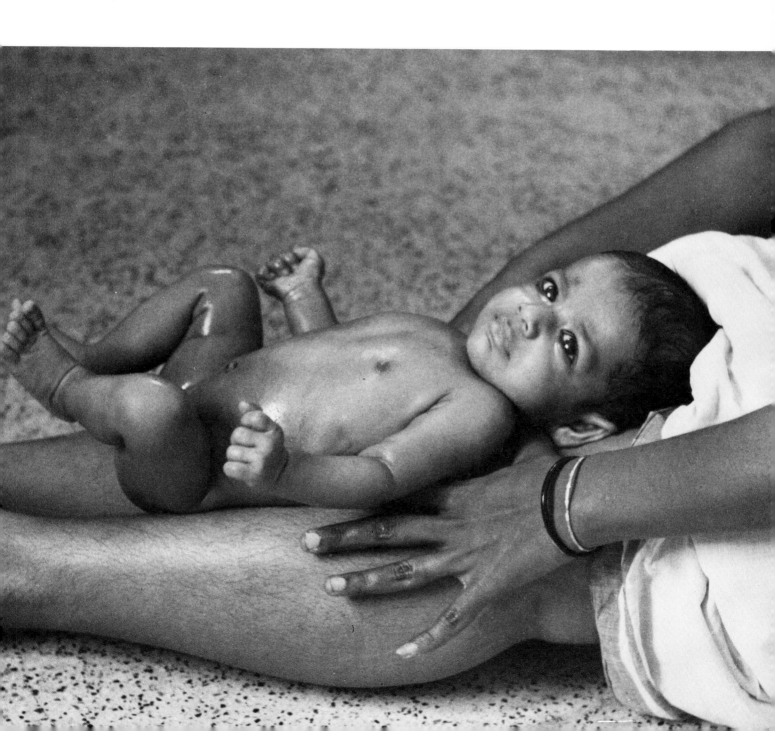

This is a Borzoi book
published by Alfred A. Knopf

Library of Congress Catalog Card Number: 75-36820
ISBN: 0-394-40469-6

Manufactured in the United States of America
Published June 9, 1976
Reprinted Four Times
Sixth Printing, October 1982

This book I dedicate
to my mother.
To all mothers.
And, of course, to Shantala.
To Shantala and, through her,
to India
who's been
a second mother to me.

When we are born, we cry that we are come
To this great stage of fools.
—Shakespeare, *King Lear*

⌘

If we ask, not "What is life?" but, more simply, "When and where does life begin?" an answer comes naturally:

"Life begins at birth."

Which seems so obvious that it sounds like a platitude.

But . . .

Within the womb, is the fetus dead?

Of course not.

Indeed, we know today that it enjoys all kinds of sensations.

Even dreams!

And so no one, after serious reflection, can really say that "life begins at birth."

What is it, then, that does begin at the moment we are born?

What is it if not life?

⌘

Fear!

Fear and the child are born together.

Fear is our faithful companion, our twin brother, our shadow.
It will never let go its hold.
Until, remorselessly, it sees us into our grave.

I have already written about this odyssey of being born.
I have told how the baby is terrified when, emerging into the outside air, it meets with the many monsters waiting there, ready to seize upon it:
the thousand and one new sensations of the world.
And I have suggested how, with a little kindness and intelligence, we can eliminate this fear.

*"Hungry or angry? Enunciate
clearly! Speak distinctly!"
"Why, sir! Angry, hungry,
what's the difference!"*
—Fairchild

꙼

What of the days to come?

What of the weeks that follow?

The infant will have yet more monsters to face.

That is to say, further new sensations.

Coming from within this time.

Sensations never experienced before. Totally new. And, therefore, terrifying.

For what is fear but the unknown?

Life was so rich within the womb!

Rich in noises and sounds. Both from the mother's body and from the outside world.

But mostly there was movement.

Continuous movement.

When the mother sits, stands, walks, turns—movement, movement, movement . . .

All pleasant, comforting sensations for the small creature inside.

And when the mother is quiet, either sitting or lying down, even when she goes to sleep, her steady, sure breathing keeps on, rocking the little traveler inside her, gently, continuously.

All day and all night, the endless flow of sensations and movements. But now . . . !

✠

Here is the child in the cradle.
All alone.
Not a sound. Not a whisper.
And worst of all . . . there is no movement!
Everything is dead. A horrible dead feeling everywhere.
A horrible loneliness.
The world outside is dead, while, suddenly, from within . . .
What is it!
What is this "thing" inside my belly that starts to creep, to gnaw at me, to bite?
No! It is not inside!
It is out there . . .
I can hear it!
I can feel it in the dark, lurking, panting, ready to pounce on me.
Help! Help!
Mommy! Mommy!

✠

An animal! A beast!
Where?
Somewhere in the dark? Somewhere in the room?
No!
It *is* inside.
Inside!
But what is it?
A new monster!
Hunger.

Hunger a monster?

But isn't feeling hungry quite pleasant?

Don't we rather enjoy it, several times a day?

Yes, it is pleasant . . . for us. Since we know that food of some kind or other will be coming.

But for the baby?

When this "terrible thing within" suddenly begins tearing at him, what can he do?

Can he go to the kitchen?

Or to a restaurant?

Can he just call "Waiter! Waiter!"

He does call actually:

"Mommy! Mommy!"

In the only language he knows:

He cries, he screams.

And most of the time, no one even cares to answer.

❡

Inside, the terrible "gnawing thing,"

and the remedy, the satisfaction . . . somewhere . . . outside.

Inside and outside.

Space is born.

And suffering.

Inside, outside: two.

That come together. Yes. But often so clumsily.

Two . . .

Oneness is lost.

Forever.

Inside and outside.

And, in between,

waiting.

Waiting, which is pain.

Waiting, which is agony.

Waiting, which is

Time.

And so it is
that Time and Space
are born
with appetite.

Yes, if a baby starts crying the moment it wakes up, it is not because
it is starving.
It is because of the newness, the strangeness of its condition.
And the contrast:
this new, terrible gnawing thing *inside,*
and the stillness, the deadness, *outside.*
A baby's belly is hungry.
No doubt.
But its skin is just as hungry.
Its skin is craving,
and so is its back,
and so is its spine,
craving for touch, craving for sensations.
Just as its belly
craves for milk.

✠

One should never forget how the baby's back had so much fun in
the womb.
I have written already about how it felt before birth.
I have told how the little one, at first, was frightened by the contrac-
tions.
But then got used to them.
Little by little began to like them.
Until it loved them and longed for them.
And I have told of the unbearable feeling of void the child experi-
ences being born: Suddenly there is nothing more to hold its body and
support its back.

The terrible, awe-inspiring scream of birth
is nothing but the expression of this sudden, unbearable, maddening nothingness—
which is simply *no touching, nothing along my back!*

✵

Therefore, if we keep in mind that waking and being born are very similar
(parting with one world
coming into another)
can we be surprised that babies start crying the very moment they wake up?
The whole contrast of birth is there again. And its terror:
nothing *talks* to their backs
nothing *outside*
and making it worse!
the terrible gnawing thing *inside.*
Nothing *outside*
everything *inside!*
Complete reverse.
The world is mad!

This is why we must caress, we must rock babies.
And, even better, massage their bodies
that are so empty, so hungry "outside."
Feeding babies with touches, giving food to their skins and their backs, is just as important as filling their stomachs.
It makes *outside* happy.
Inside and *outside* satisfied. . . .
No more two.
Oneness again.
And peace.

✠

    Yes, we should not forget that the five senses are one. And all of them extensions of the skin.

    They are, in a way, the fingers of the brain, feeling, exploring the world outside.

    They open one by one, reaching further and further. Expanding the universe. Enriching it.

    The sense of smell reaches far beyond where the hand can go.

    Hearing goes further still.

    And seeing . . . To see is to caress the whole world with the eyes.

    But everything starts with touching.

    Language, which "knows" far more than we realize, holds memories of this. Don't we say:

    "I tried to get in touch."

    "Oh, how touching!"

✠

    Touching, yes, is the root.
    It must be dealt with accordingly.

    We have to feed babies,
    fill them both
    inside and outside.

    We must speak to their skins,
    we must speak to their backs,
    which thirst and hunger
    and cry
    as much as their bellies.

    We must gorge them
    with warmth and caresses
    just as we do with milk.

Being touched and caressed,
being massaged,
is food for the infant.
Food as necessary
as minerals, vitamins, and proteins.
Deprived of this food,
the name of which is love,
babies would rather die.
And they often do.

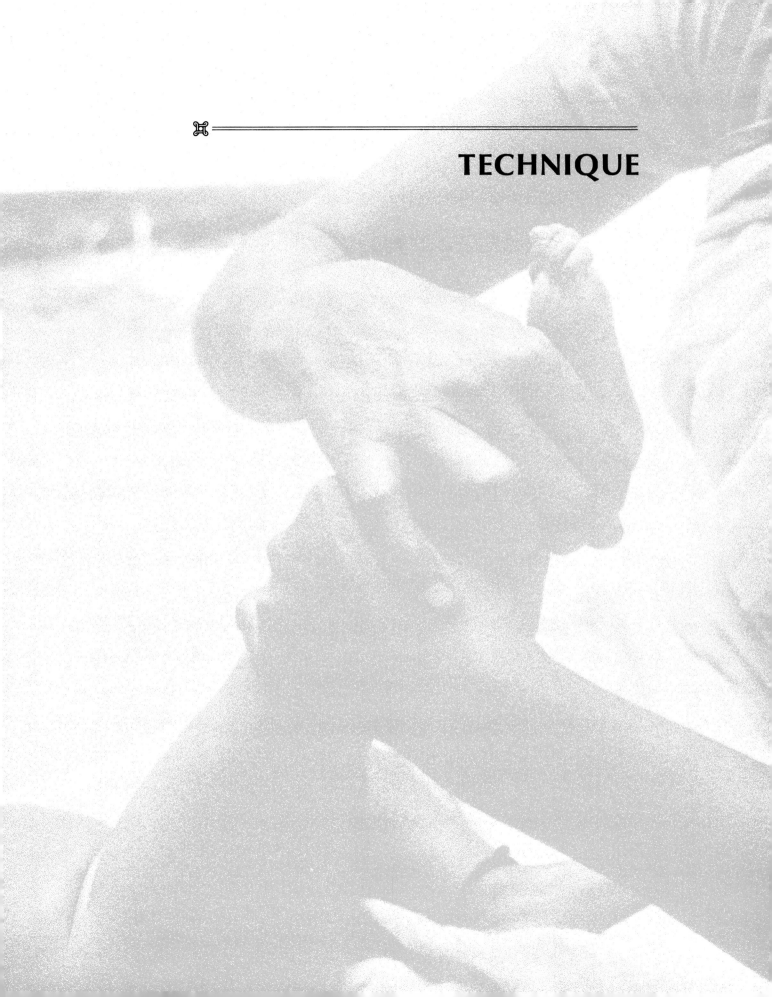

TECHNIQUE

Ⓗ

Ⓗ

Massaging a baby is an art.
As deep as it is old.
And yet so simple.
Simple but difficult.
And difficult *because* simple.
Women in India learn it from their mothers.

Then, someday, they teach it to their daughters, who in turn will teach *their* daughters, who then . . .

It is a sacred art, in the true sense, since it is concerned with babies, with the renewal of life.

Any art has its technique,
which one must learn.
Of course there is much more to "art" than technique,
and in time you will come to it.
Once technique has been fully mastered . . .
and forgotten.

But before we forget, we must first learn.
So let us begin with technique.

The child must be completely naked.
Therefore it is important that the room be pleasantly warm.

In summertime, in warm countries, massaging can be done outdoors.
 And afterward the child will be left in the sun for a short while, its
head carefully protected by a parasol or shade of some kind.

You should use oil—
In winter, it should be warmed.
In India, women use mustard oil in winter, coconut oil in summer.
Olive oil, almond oil may do as well.

Never massage a child whose stomach is full,
which is to say never right after you have been feeding the child.

After the massage, you will bathe the child.
And we will tell you about it later.

In the first month of the baby's life, the massaging has to be exqui-sitely gentle.
It is just the touching all over that the baby loves,
and when you begin, if the baby wants to cry a little—
let it cry—
it is a baby's way of talking.
But soon it should settle down
into deep enjoyment.

The mother should sit down on the floor.
This is essential.
No table.
And no chair.
Otherwise the profound significance and benefit of the massaging will be lost.
For both the mother
and the baby.

And now you are ready.
Next to you there is oil in a little container.
You have laid a towel over your extended legs.
It must be a thick towel, since your baby may empty its bladder, utterly relaxed by its feeling of profound well-being.

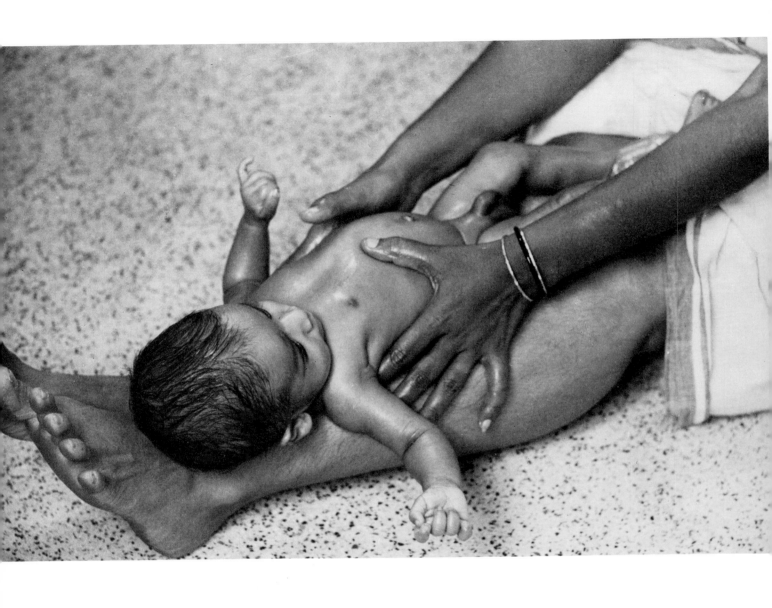

Or you may prefer to lay your baby right on your naked legs.

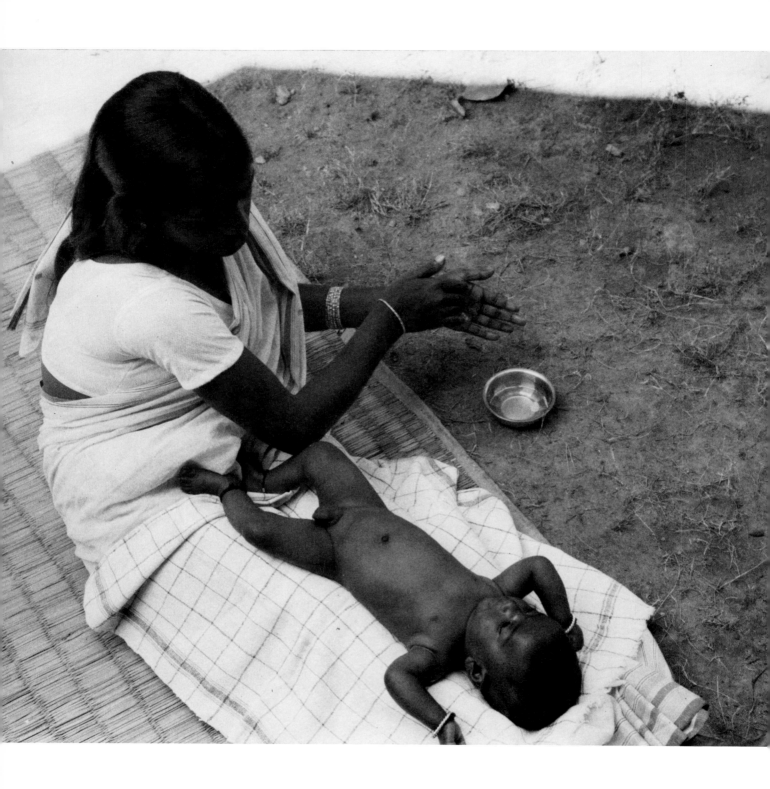

✠

Here you are, looking at each other.

At every moment, your massaging must be sensitive and responsive to the slightest flutter of this new being.

You will be holding an unbroken dialogue.

Not in words, of course!

True communication, true communion, is silent, as you know.

Speak with your eyes.

Speak through your hands.

Let it all flow from your heart.

Be *here*, live *now*, completely!

For if your mind is on other things, the baby will know it immediately.

The whole thing would become purely mechanical, a mere exercise. Easy, boring, and empty.

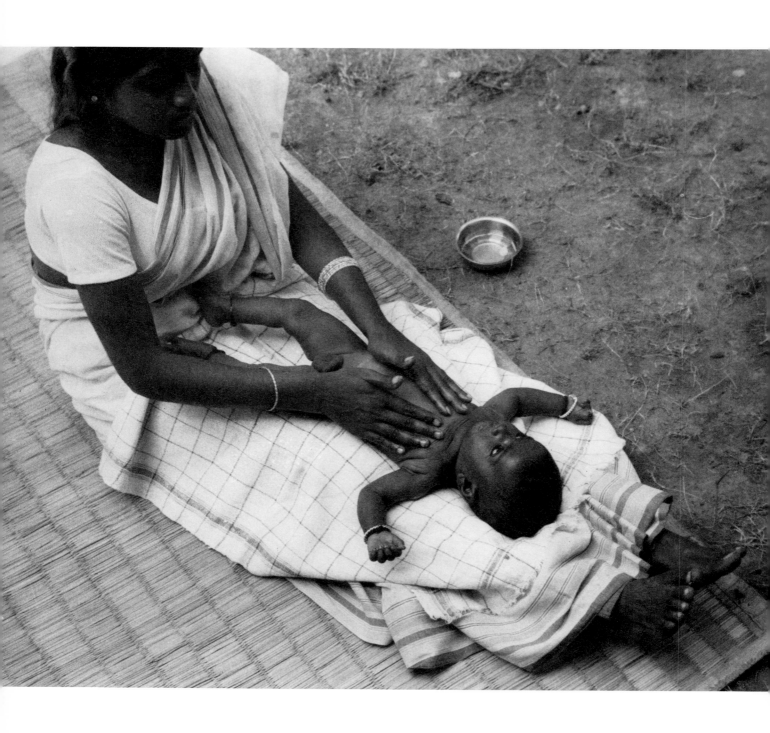

THE CHEST

Put some oil on your hands.

Then apply a little of this oil to your baby's chest.

And start moving your hands gently and slowly out to both sides. Very gently. And very very slowly.

Come back to the middle of the chest and start again, your hands more or less following the line of your baby's ribs.

Both your hands are working together, although moving in opposite directions.

As if smoothing flat the pages of a book open in front of you.

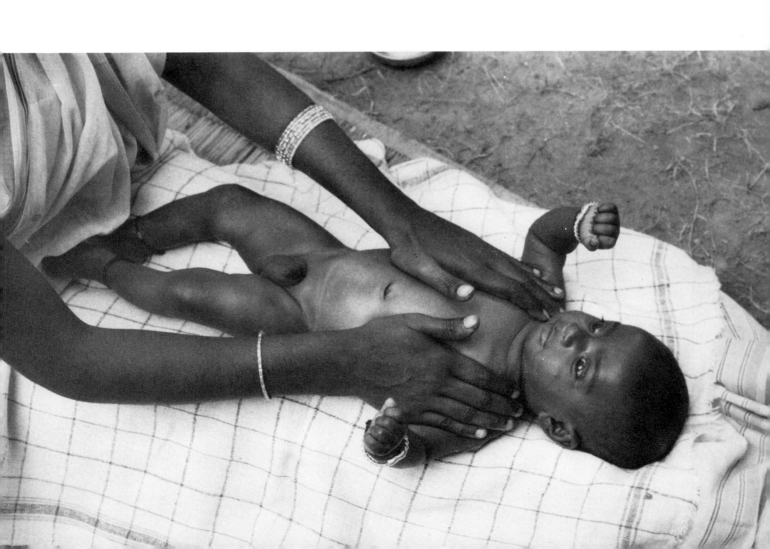

Now your hands are going to work *one after the other.*

Your right hand starts from your baby's flank, and moves across the chest toward the *opposite* shoulder.

The moment this right hand reaches the shoulder, your left hand begins its motion, from the opposite side of your baby's abdomen, moving across the chest until it reaches the opposite shoulder.

Then your right hand, starting again from . . .

And on and on, your hands moving one after the other, like waves . . .

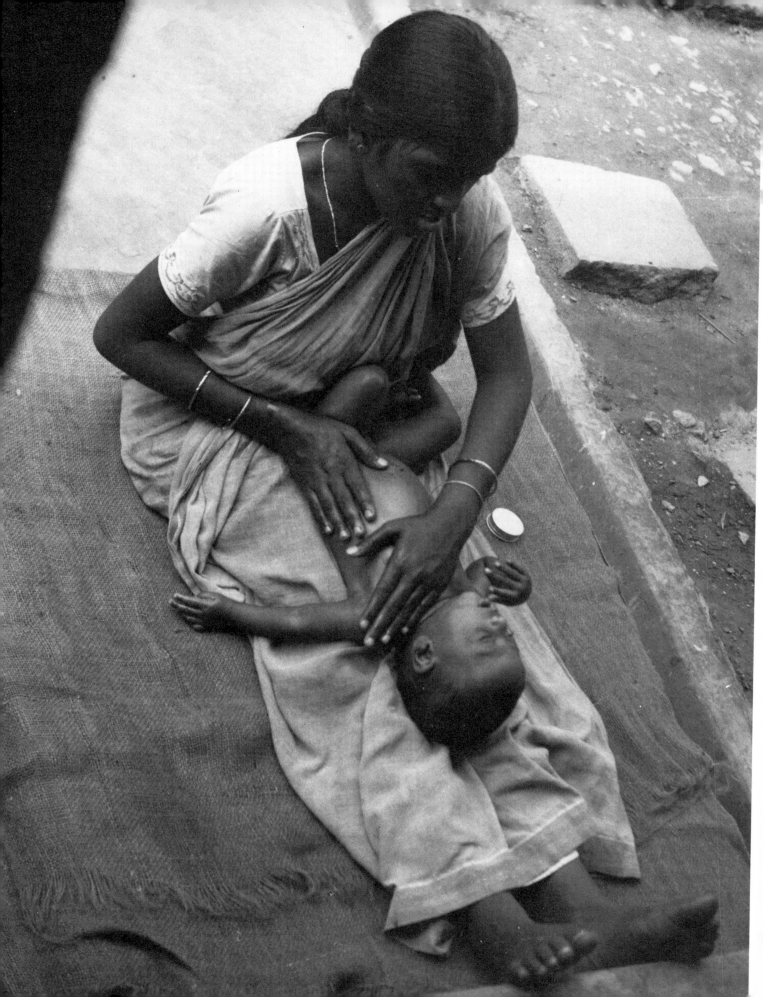

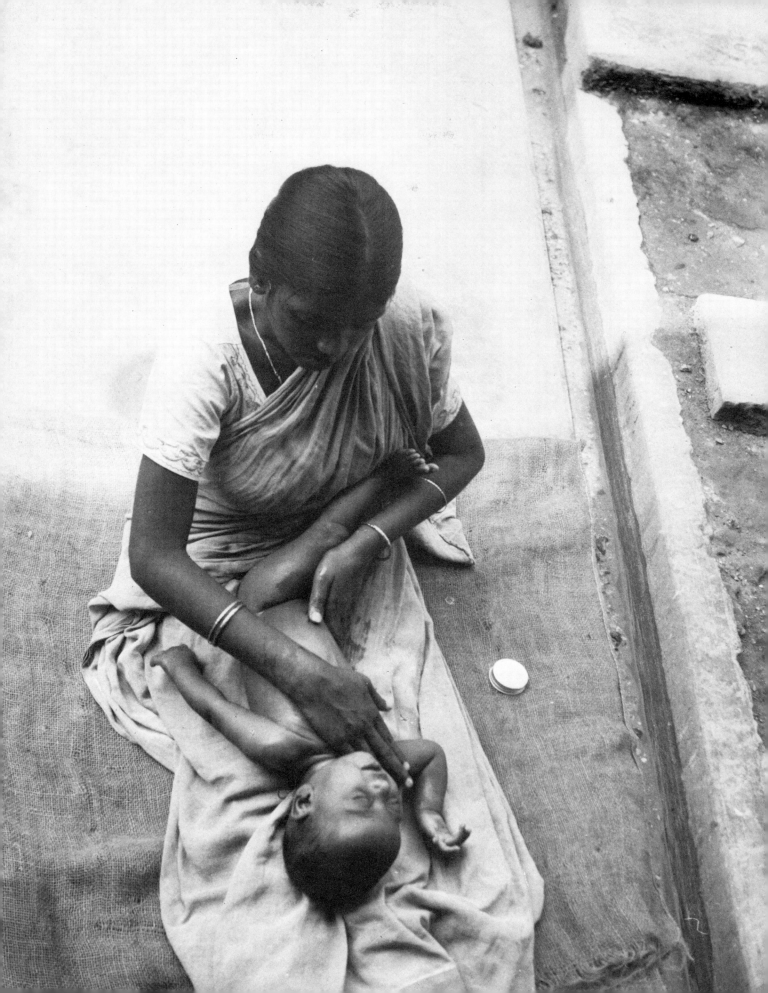

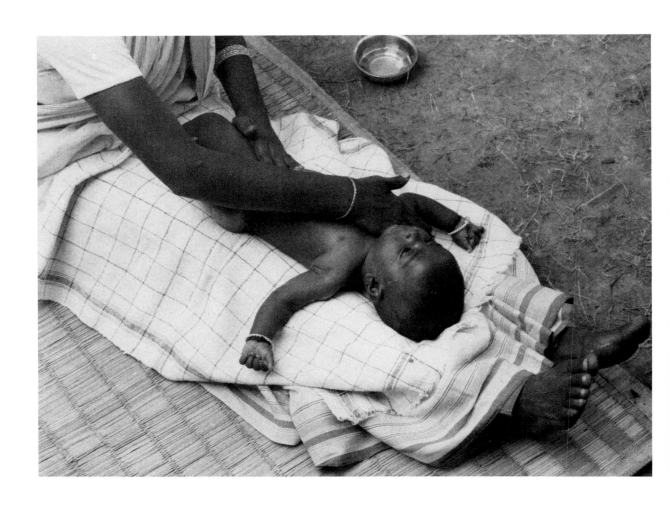

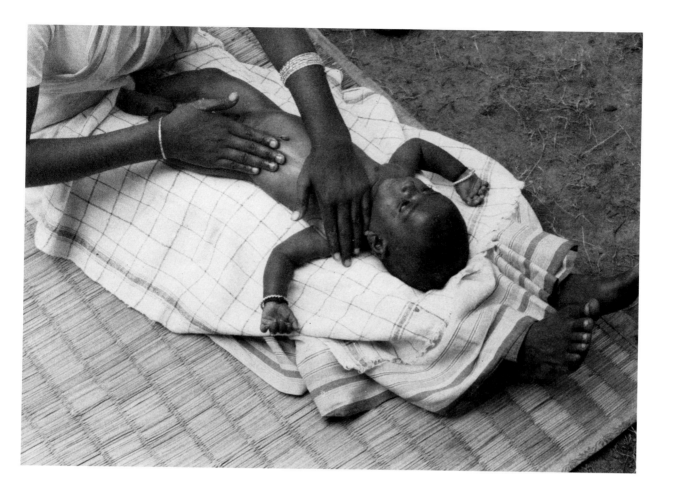

You started slowly, lightly.

Never accelerating the movement, keeping the rhythm very slow (You are *never* to accelerate. Maintaining a slow, regular rhythm is essential!),

the pressure of your hands becomes stronger.

It is not a conscious act.

It simply happens, instinctively.

And notice that when your hand reaches the shoulder, it moves right along the neck of your baby.

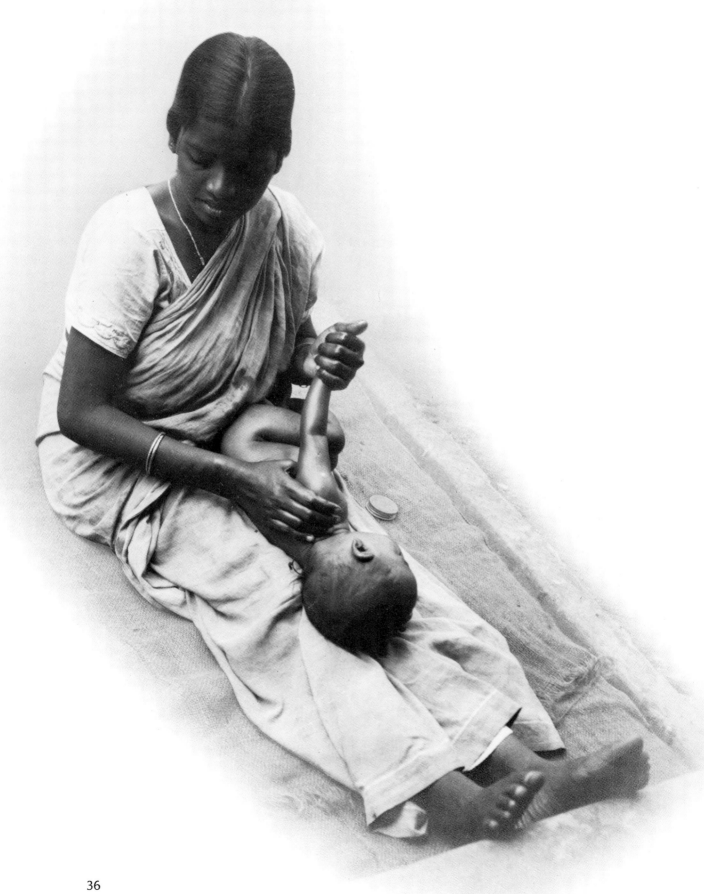

✠

THE ARMS

Now you turn your baby on one side. And begin massaging the arms.
Suppose you start with the left arm. As Shantala does in the picture.
With your left hand holding the wrist, you extend your baby's arm.

Then your right hand grasps the shoulder, and moves slowly along your infant's arm.

Your fingers form a tight little bangle, and "milk" the limb. Not downward but upward.

The moment your right hand reaches your baby's wrist, your left hand, which had been holding it, becomes free and grasps the shoulder, and moves upward along the arm. Now *it* reaches the wrist, setting your right hand free.

Which, in turn, grasps the shoulder . . .

The movements are rhythmic, soothing.

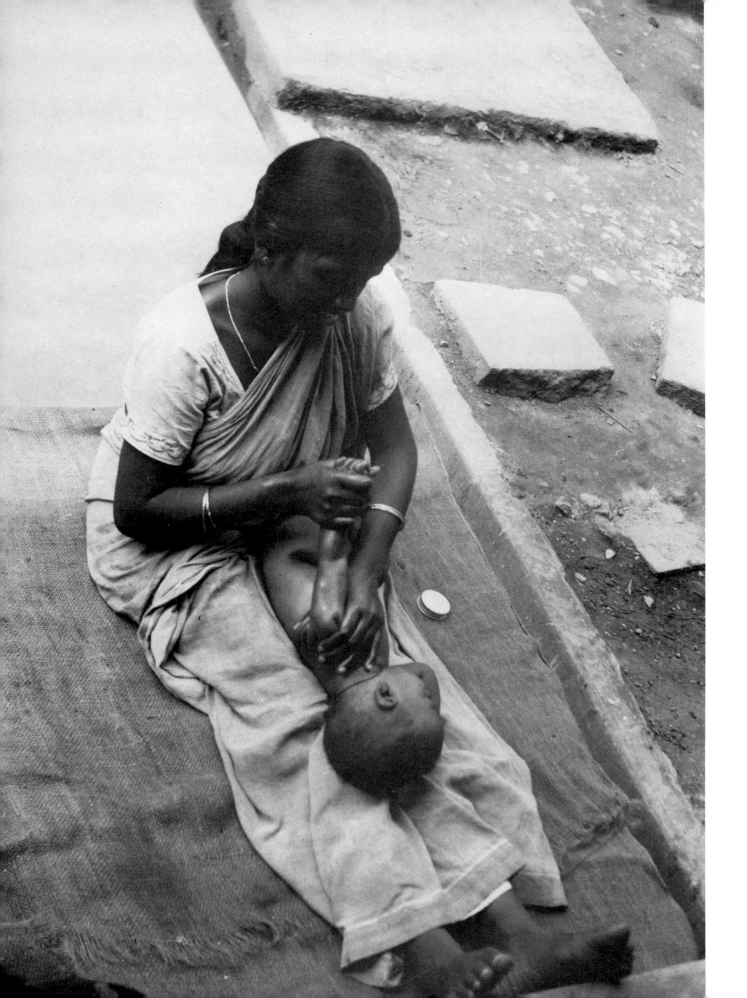

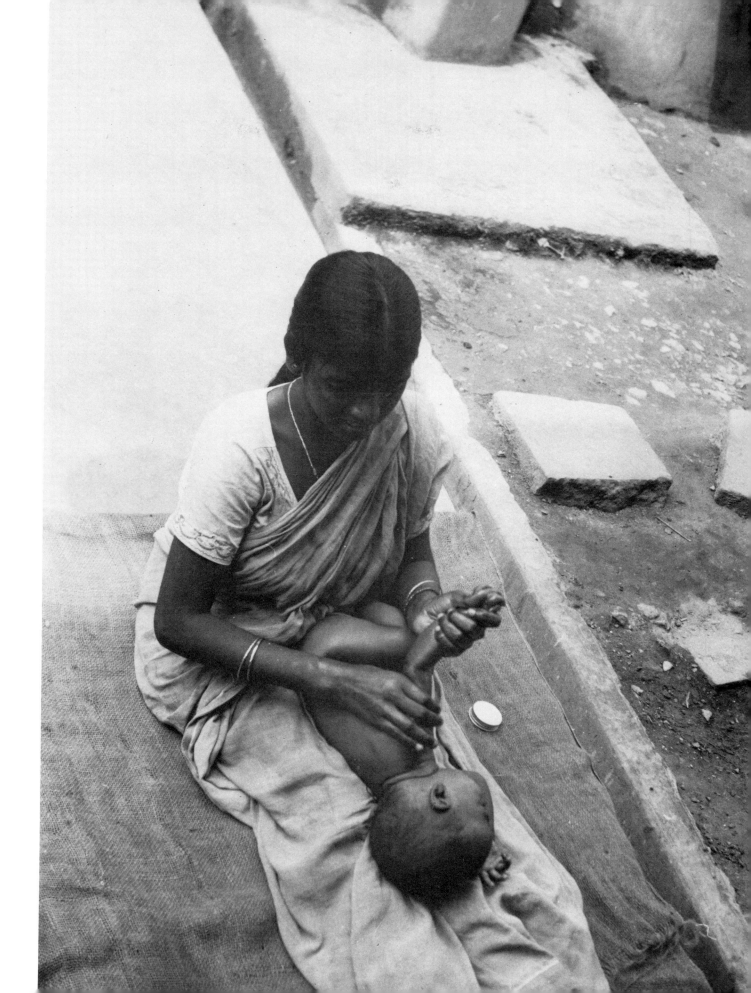

Your hands have been working one after the other. Now they are to work together.

40

They both grasp your baby's shoulder and, moving circularly and in opposite directions (a benign form of twisting and squeezing the arm), they progress toward the hand.

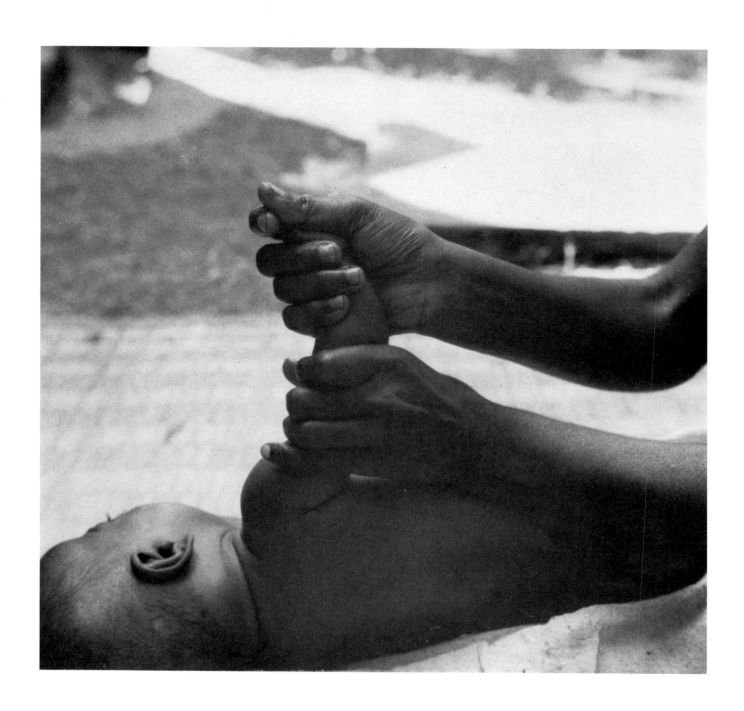

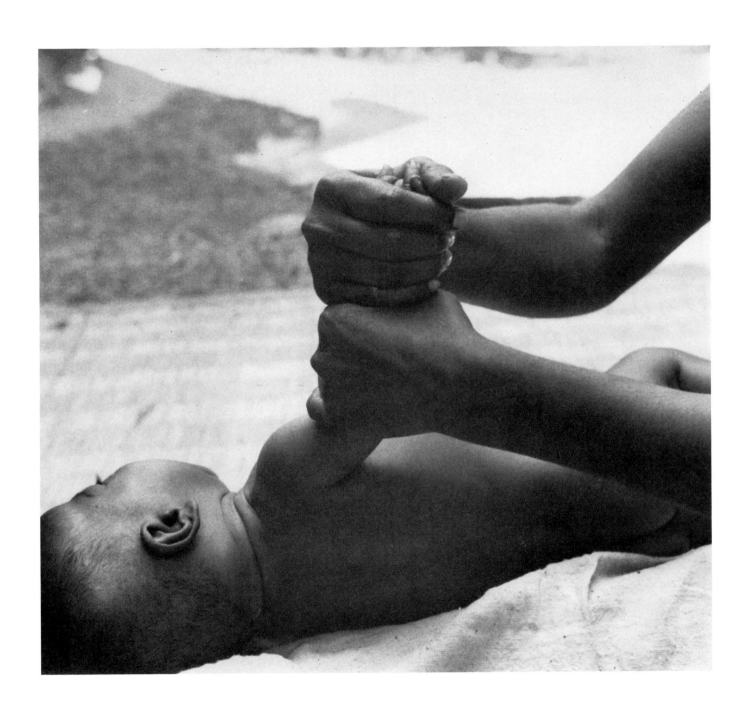

Once they reach it, they return to the shoulder, grasp it, and . . .

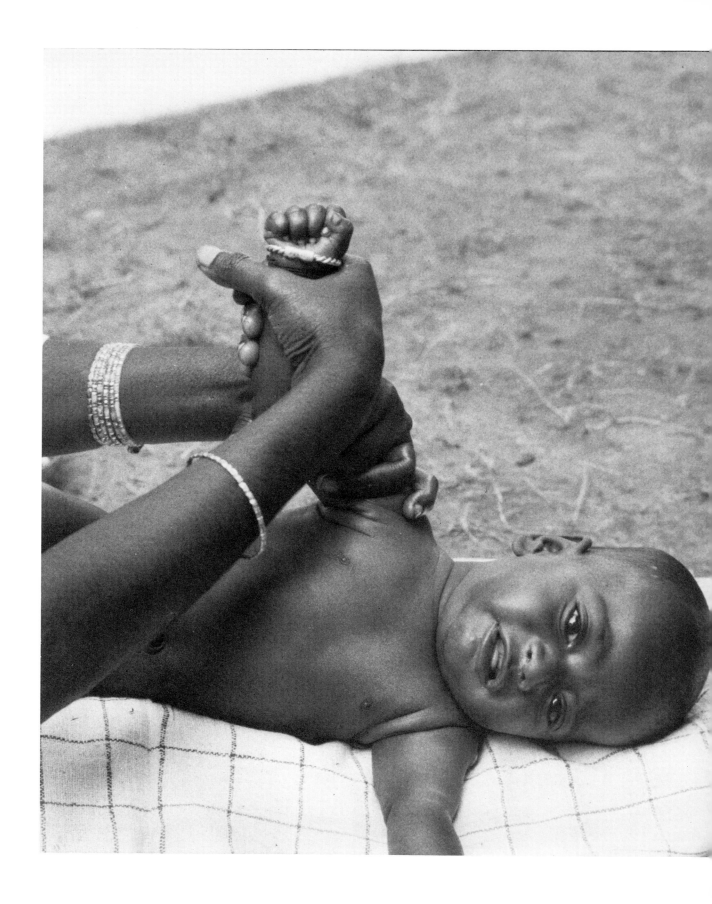

Your baby's wrists are sensitive and important.
Your hands have to work longer on them.

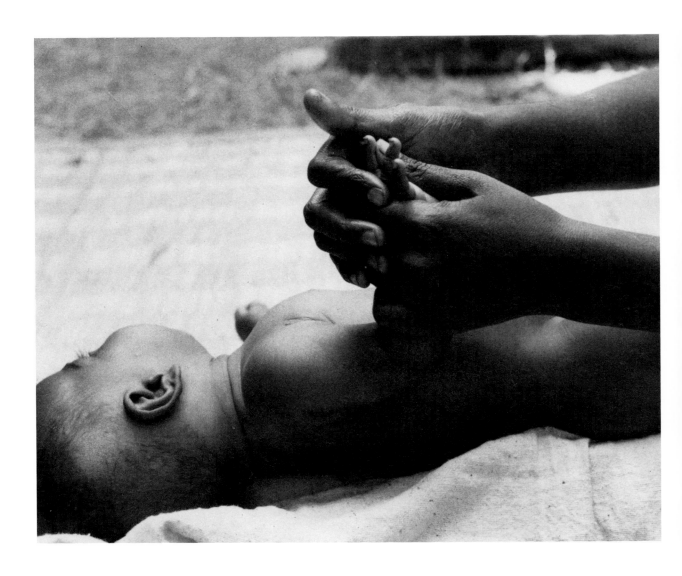

✠
THE HANDS

Now, with both your hands holding the wrist, your two thumbs working one after the other, start massaging the palm of the hand toward the fingers.

Once this is done, massage the fingers—unfolding them again and again.

And then, of course, you repeat all of this with the other arm, after turning the child on its opposite side.

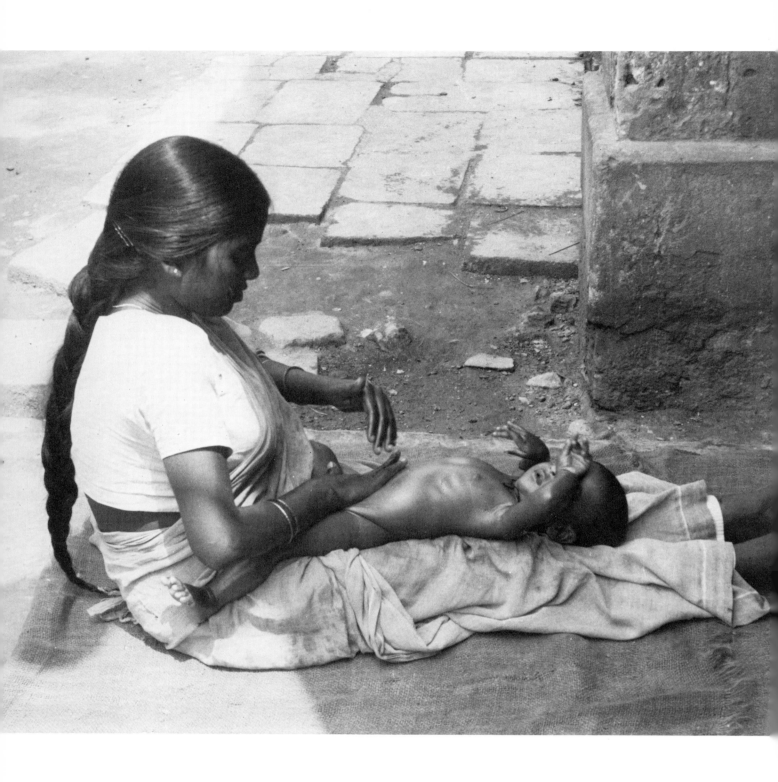

✠
THE ABDOMEN

Now your child is lying on its back again.

Both your hands, working one after the other, massage the belly.

Starting from the base of the little chest, your hands move downward toward yourself, one after the other.

As if to empty the stomach.

And, now, with your left hand, grasp your baby's feet and stretch its legs upward.

Thus the abdomen relaxes.

And your massaging goes deeper.

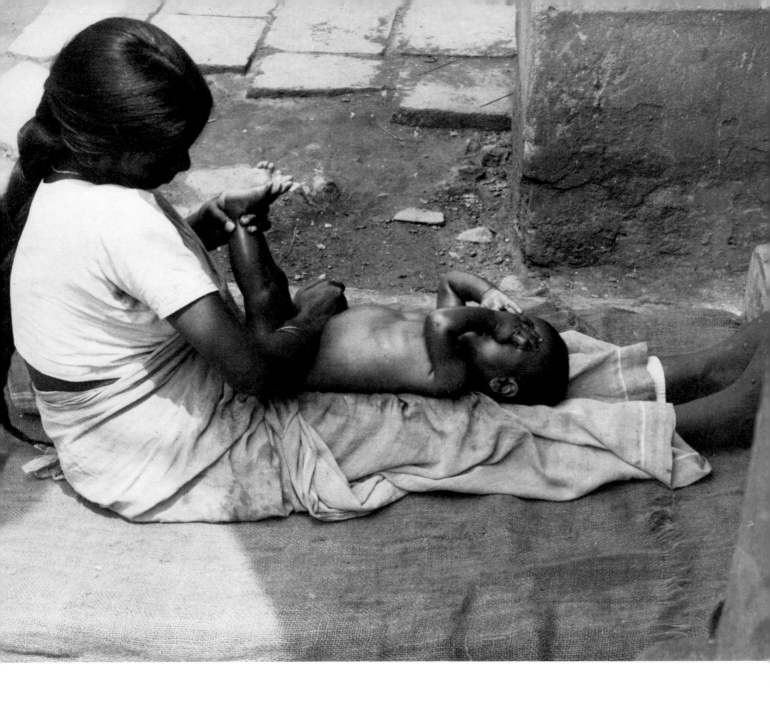

✠
THE LEGS

Now the legs.

Proceed exactly as you did with the arms, although you need not turn the baby on its side.

So, keeping the infant lying on its back, first grasp the left thigh with one hand while your other hand holds the foot and stretches the leg.

Move first one hand upward like a small tight bangle.

Then the other.

And again . . .

As if "milking" the leg upward.

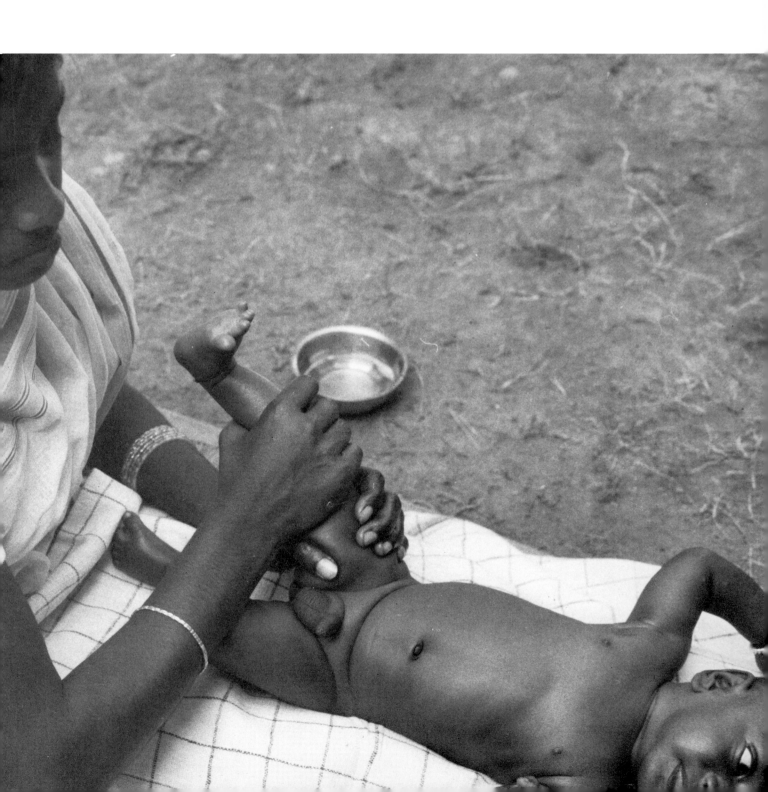

Your hands have been working one after the other. Now they work together, moving upward in circles along the leg.

Do not forget that your baby's ankles are just as important as the wrists; you must massage them with special attention.

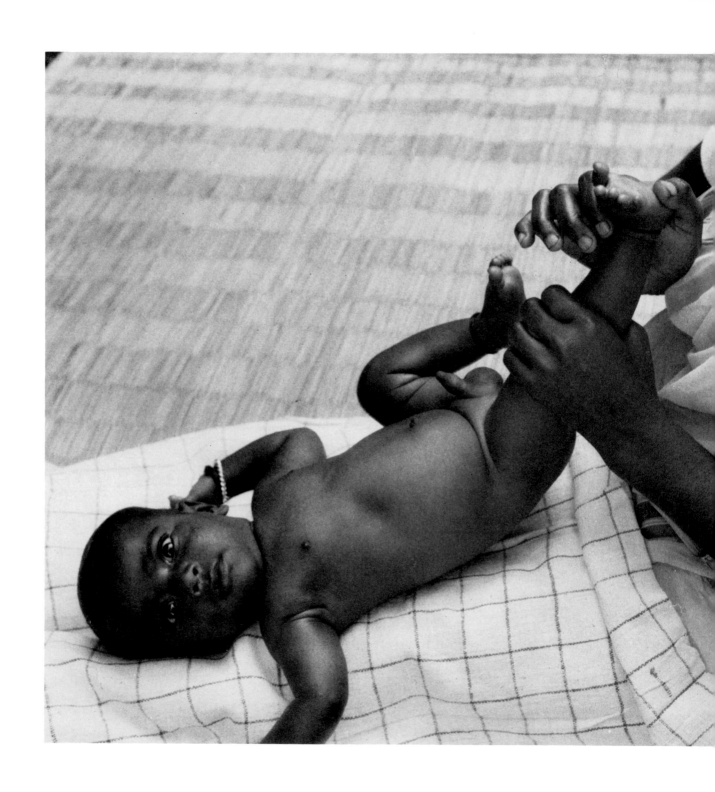

And, now, the foot.
First with your thumbs . . .

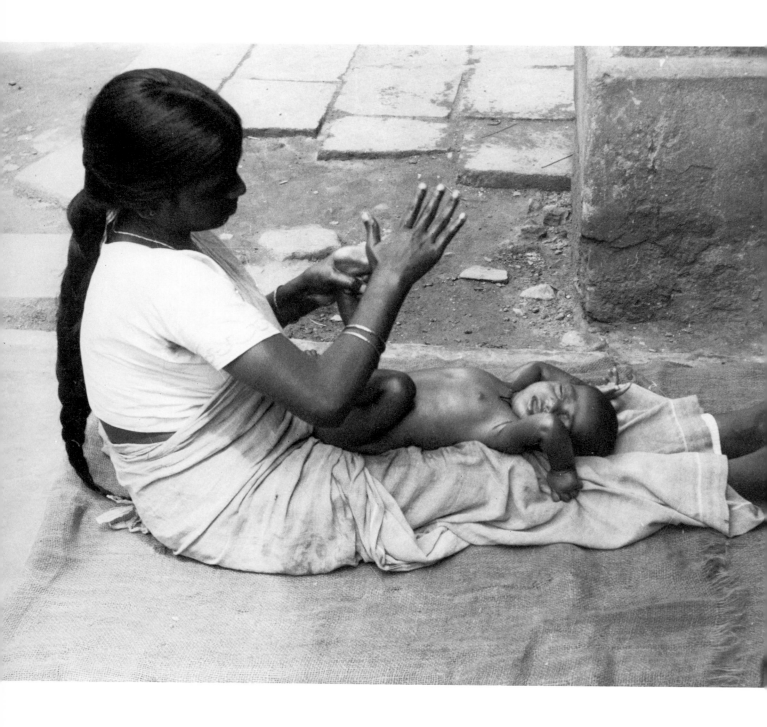

Then with the palm of one hand.

And, of course, once you have finished the left leg you do all the same things with the right.

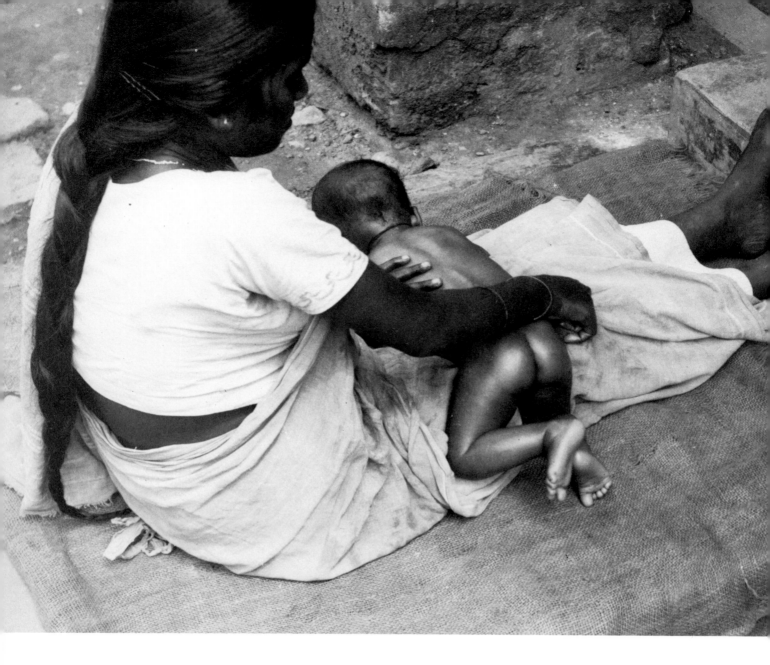

THE BACK

Now you are going to massage your baby's back.

Which is, perhaps, the most important part of all.

The massaging of the body must be a unity, with no part ignored or neglected.

But give extra time to the back.

And all your attention.

Lift your child, turn it over on its tummy and place it across your legs with its head to your left.

Back massaging is done in three steps.

First:

✵

Across the back

Your left hand moves forward across the back
then backward toward you
then forward again.

The right hand moves forward the moment the left hand starts moving backward.

Thus both hands work together, across the back, but in opposite directions.

Now, as your hands move to and fro, forward and backward,
little by little they also progress from your left to your right.

You start your massaging near the head of the baby.

And slowly you move down the back.

Your hands, continually going forward and backward, progress from the shoulders to the upper back, then to the small of the back, ending over the buttocks.

Then, up again toward the shoulders, over the small of the back, the upper back, ultimately reaching the point where you began.

And then down again—from left to right.

You combine two movements here:

the to and fro movements of your hands across the back

and the progression along the baby's back, up and down, almost as if you were playing scales on the piano.

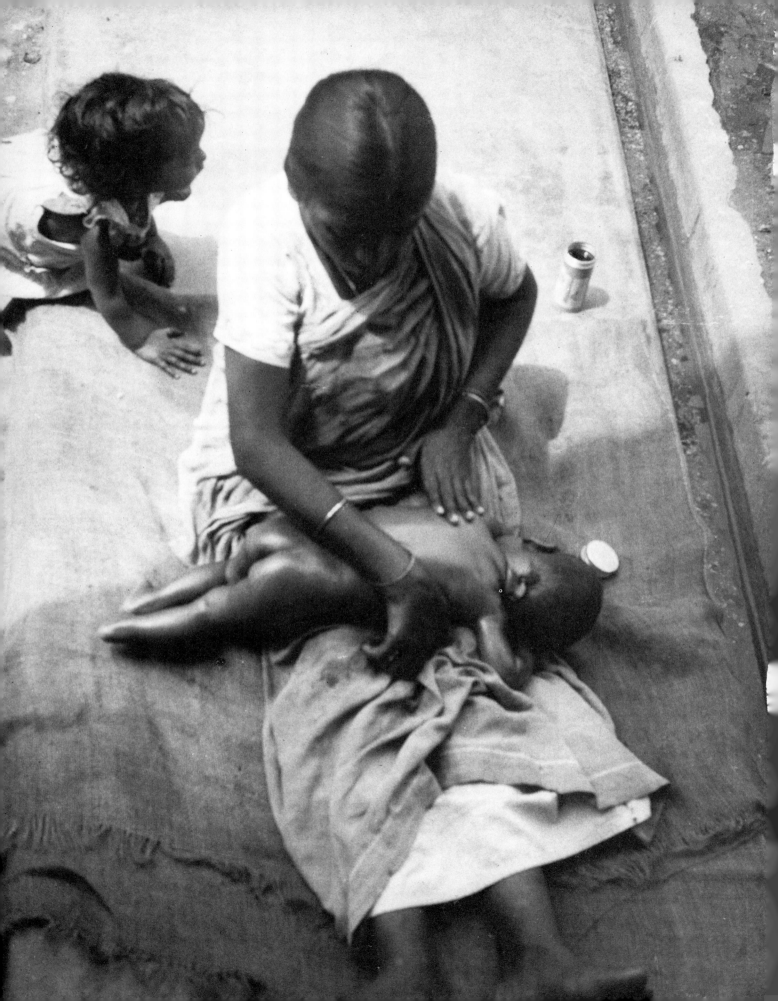

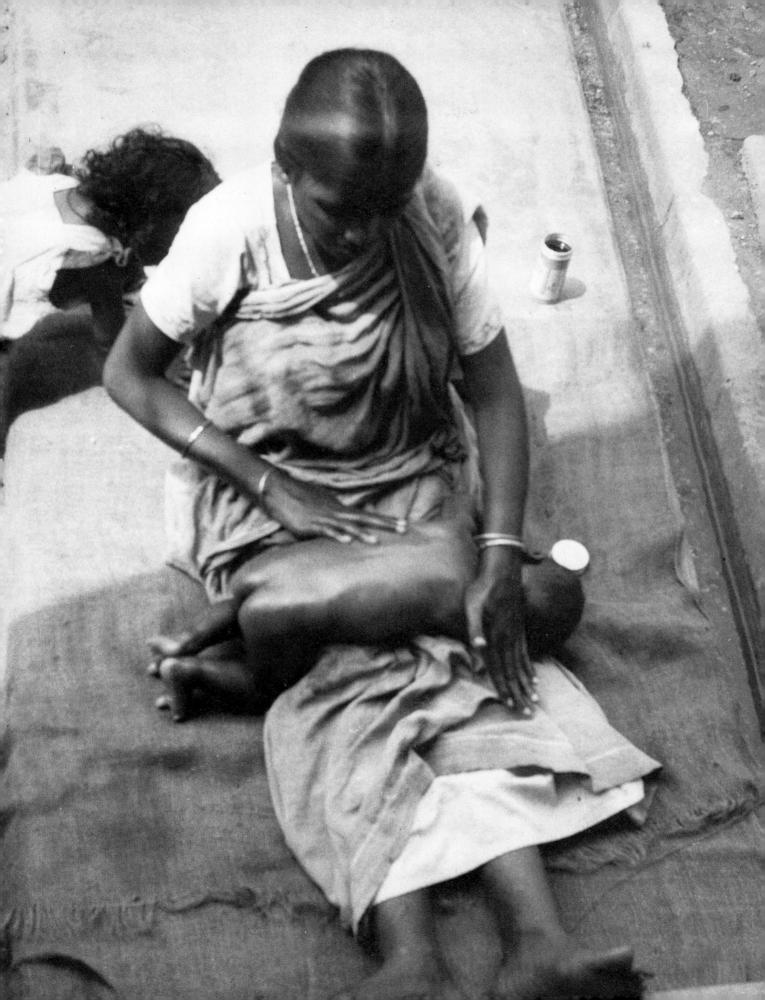

✠

Down, along the back

Both your hands have been working, one after the other.

Now your left hand is going to move alone,

not across the back of the baby, but down, along the spine.

With continuity: without a break, either in the pressure or in . . . your concentration!

Keep summoning up your energy, although as slowly as you can.

This is where your mastery will show: The more slowly you massage, the deeper the sensations.

But this vital energy of yours has to be totally free from violence or aggression.

A fact worth pondering.

While your left hand keeps moving down, along your baby's back,
your right hand holds its bottom firmly.
So that, actually, both your hands are working.
But in this case the left hand stands for dynamic energy
while the right hand represents static energy.
Both of your hands and these twin aspects of energy are working in
perfect harmony.

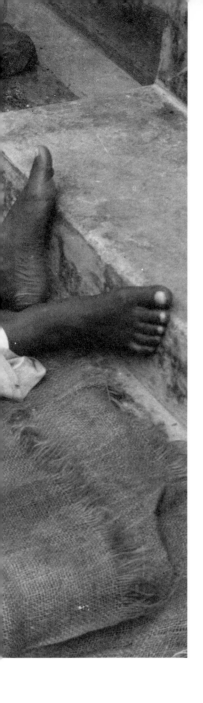

⌘

Down to the heels

Your right hand now grasps your baby's feet, so that your left hand, instead of stopping at the buttocks, goes right on down to the heels.

In one long beautiful movement.

Remember that your right hand is to grasp both feet delicately, keeping your baby's legs extended.

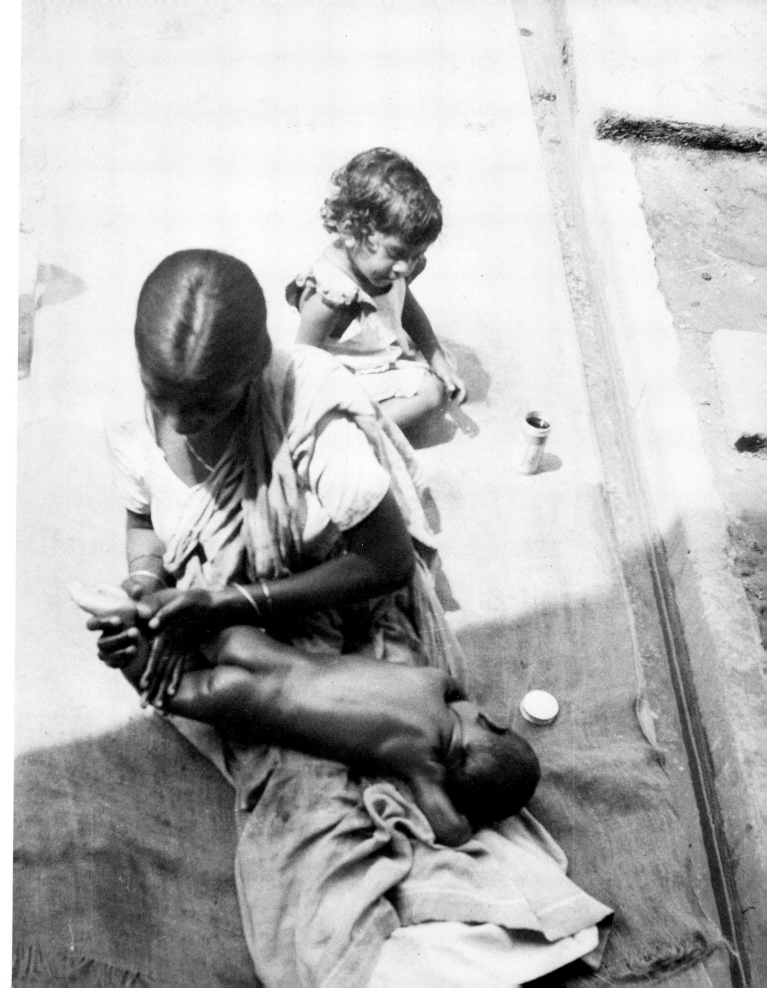

✠

The massaging of the back is now over.

It was the most important part of all, since it is along the spine that tensions often build up and remain unnoticed.

They are quite easy to release at this young age.

But more and more difficult as time goes by.

And unless dealt with at this time of life, they can remain forever.

Turning the proudest of living creatures into inner cripples.

As you can see by looking at people around you!

Which is why it is wise to take plenty of time when you massage your baby's precious back. And to give your full concentration.

Now lift the child and place it on its back again.

Not across your legs now, but along them.

Now you are to massage . . .

THE FACE

You start with . . .

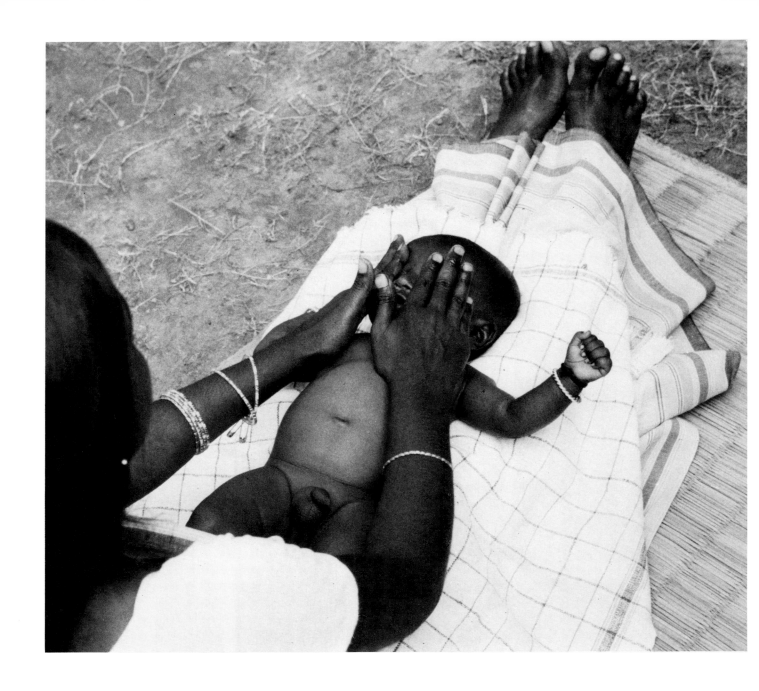

The forehead

Starting from the middle of the forehead, the tips of your fingers
move sideways, along the eyebrows.

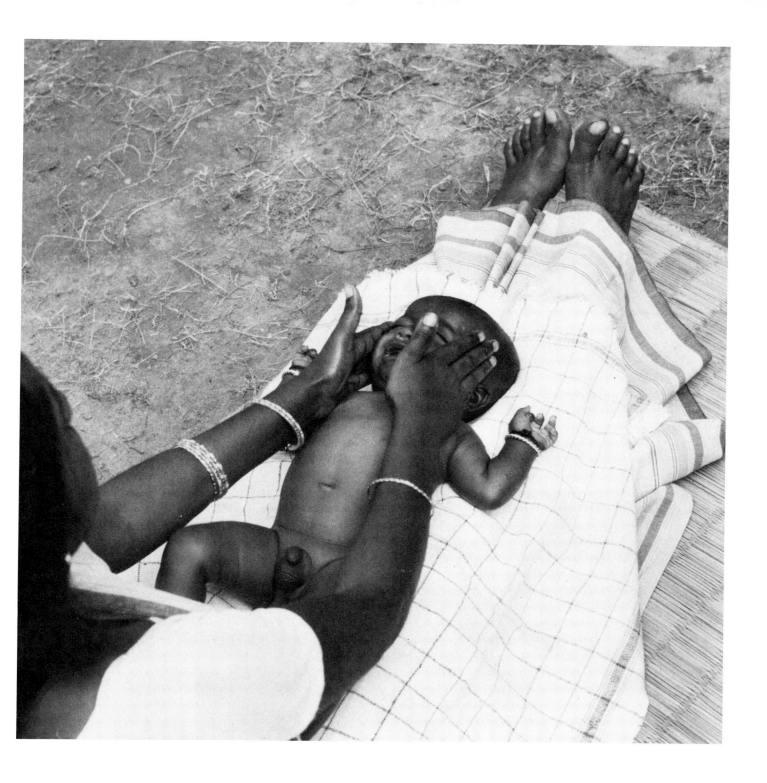

Then return to where they started from.
Move sideways again.
Then back . . .

The bridge of the nose

Both your thumbs, working together very lightly, move upward (toward the forehead) along the sides of the nose.

Then again.

And again . . .

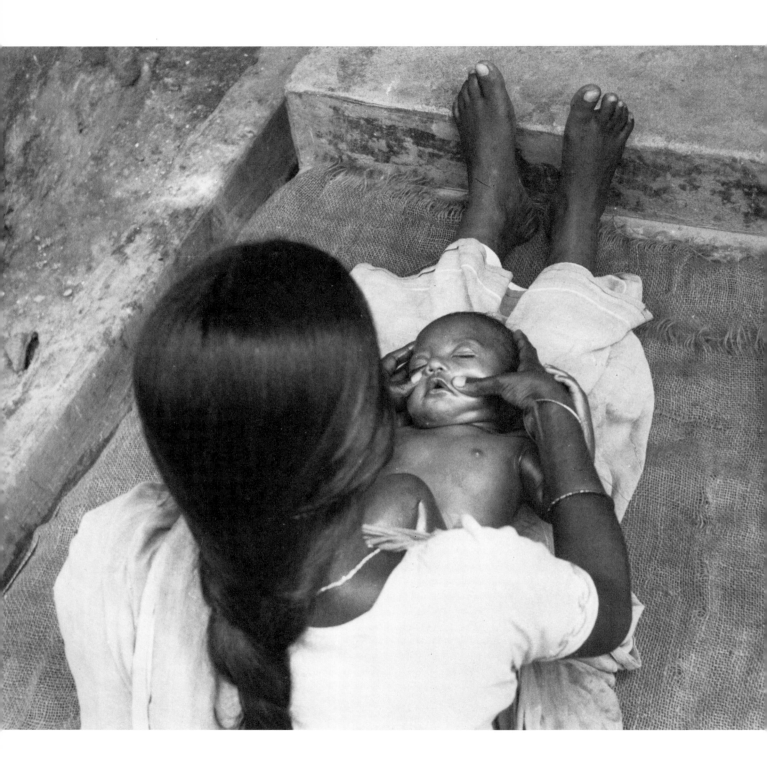

Down along the nose

Apply your thumbs very lightly to your baby's eyelids. Closed, of course.

And then move them downward. And slightly sideways, so that they slide along the nose, reach the corners of the mouth, and gently stretch the mouth out. Then back again to the eyelids . . .

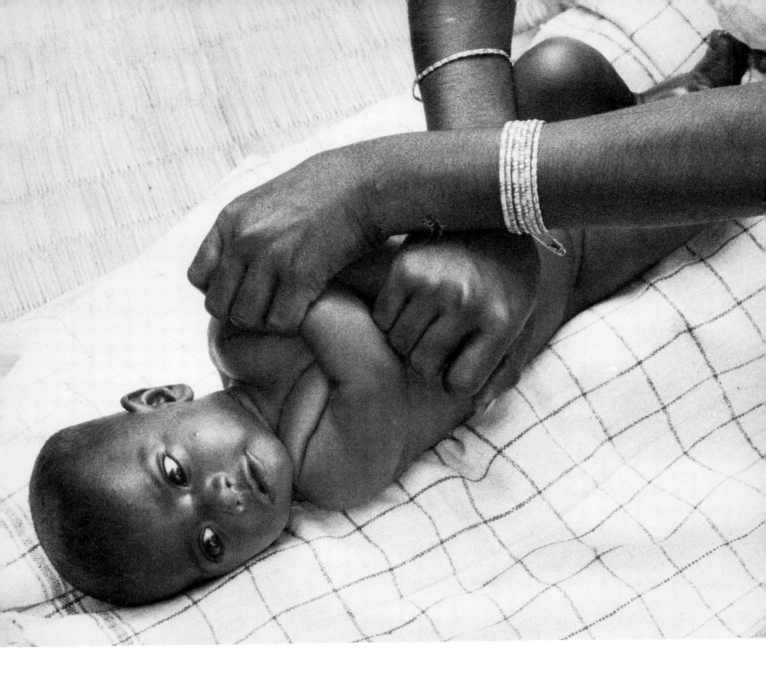

You are now going to conclude with three exercises.
One might say, three Asana or Postures.
Since we are, here, so close to Hatha-Yoga.

✠

BOTH ARMS

Each of your hands grasps one of your baby's hands. Or one of its wrists.
Fold both arms over and onto the chest.
Now open them again, stretching them out, like unfolding wings.
Then, folding, back on the chest again.
Then, open again . . .

ONE ARM AND ONE LEG

In the same way, hold one foot and the opposite hand.

Make them cross each other.

Which means that your baby's pliable little foot touches its opposite shoulder. While its hand reaches toward its buttocks.

Then bring both limbs back to where you started from.

Then repeat with the opposite hand and the opposite foot.

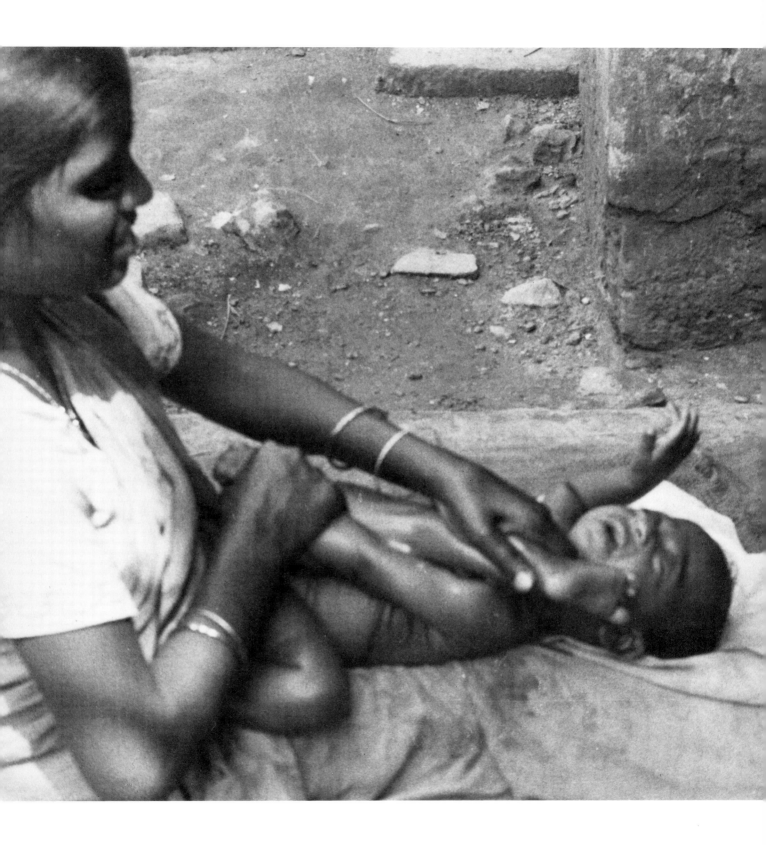

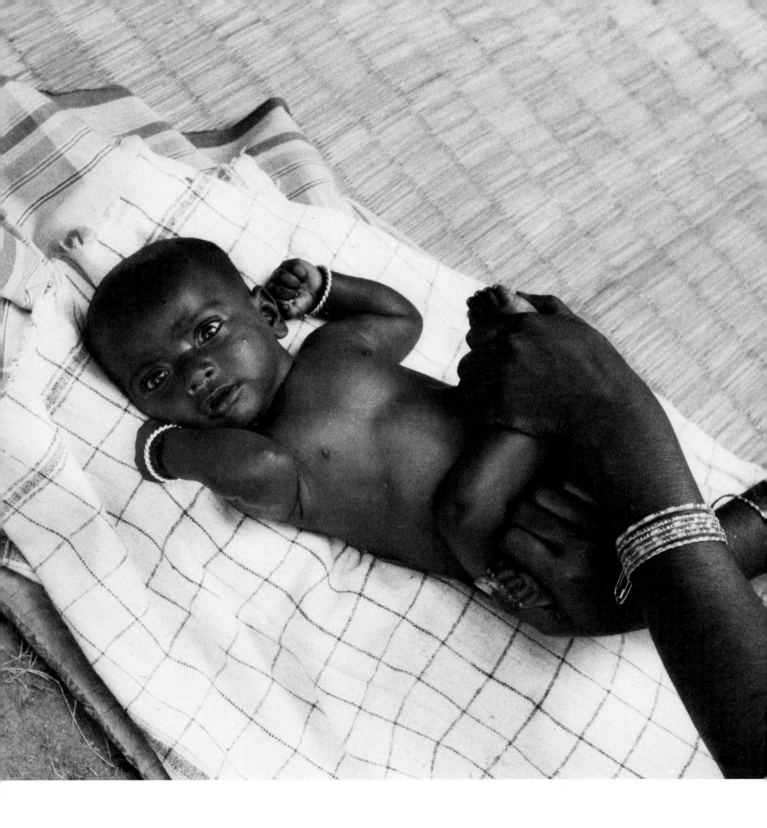

PADMASANA

Yes, the Lotus Posture!
Grasping both feet, bring both legs up to cross over the abdomen.
Then back to where you started from, stretching the legs out.
Then cross them again, gently folding them.
Then opening.
And again . . .
Very gently.
Very slowly.
But firmly.

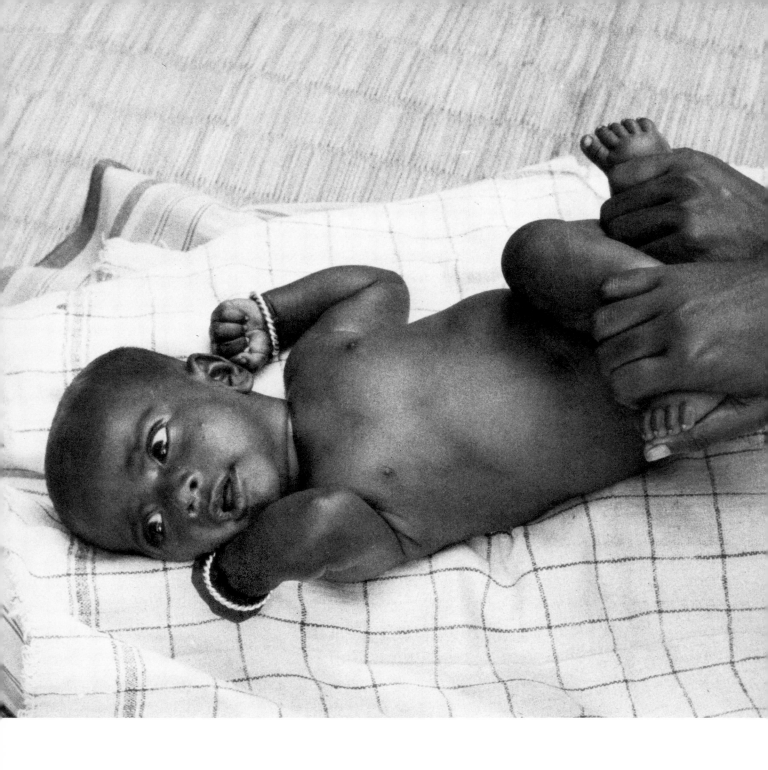

Each of these last three exercises requires great sensitivity and inborn intelligence.

Crossing the arms releases tensions along the back, freeing the chest and liberating it for better breathing.

Crossing one arm and one leg acts upon the whole of the spine, which bends sideways and rotates slightly on its axis.

Crossing both legs brings to their maximum flexibility the joints that link pelvis, sacrum, and backbone.

The basic purpose of all this is "stretching out."

These exercises act directly upon the muscles, which they extend and relax.

But their main purpose is to act upon the joints, which are made to open and function fully.

Of course these three exercises must be done very gently.

With very light and loving hands.

BACK IN WATER

The massaging is over. Now your baby is to be bathed.

Not because a good washing is necessary; all the oil has been absorbed by the skin.

No. It is not a matter of cleanliness.

But of deep well-being. Of complete freedom.

Water is going to complete your work. Make it perfect.

There may still be some tensions there, along the spine, around the pelvis. Tensions so deep that they do not betray themselves to your hands.

Water will make them simply melt away.

As the sun would the snow.

All you need to know is how.

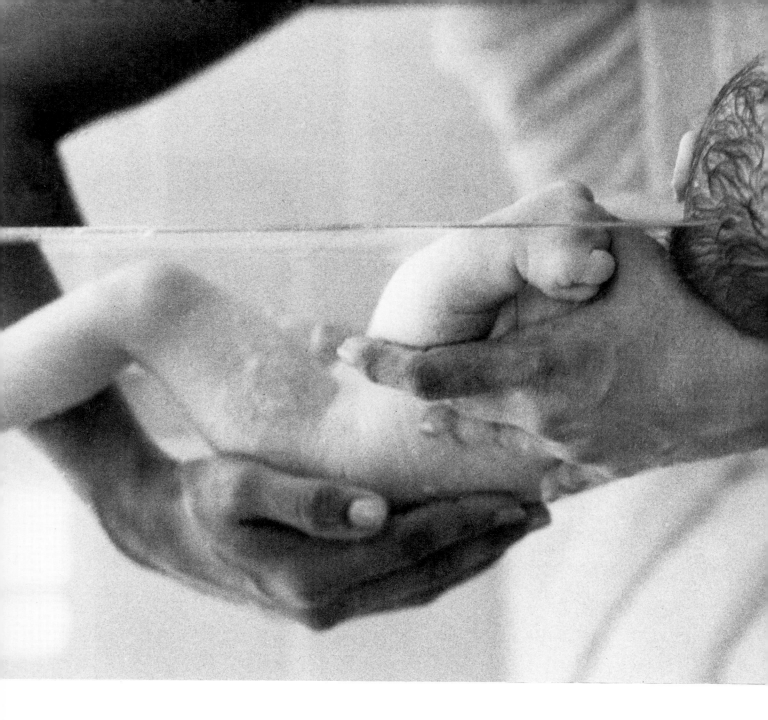

Lift your baby. Hold it under the armpits.
And very slowly and gently let the body slide into the water.
And then let your baby float.
You are facing the side of the baby's bath.
Your baby's head is to your left.
And your left hand supports your child.

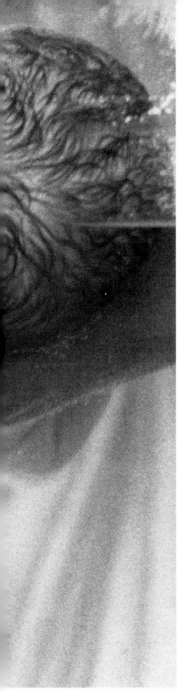

Supports, mind you.

You are not to *hold* your child.

Allow it to float.

The nape of your baby's neck will simply rest on your wrist. With your hand wide open.

Yes, wide open. This is a basic expression of your understanding. And of the profound nature of the bond between you and your child.

With your thumb and index finger wide apart, your middle finger merely acts like a hook, gently controlling the infant's armpit. Preventing the small body from slipping.

Yes, just allow the infant to float.

Be passive. Entirely passive. Although totally aware.

Do not try to direct.

Do not interfere.

Your baby is in his own element!

Don't come between them.

Let things happen.

And watch!

Watch how the whole body comes to life. And plays.

Just watch,

let it happen.

At the beginning you may not feel sure that your left hand is sufficient, so use your right hand to complement it.

Embracing the body, as it were.

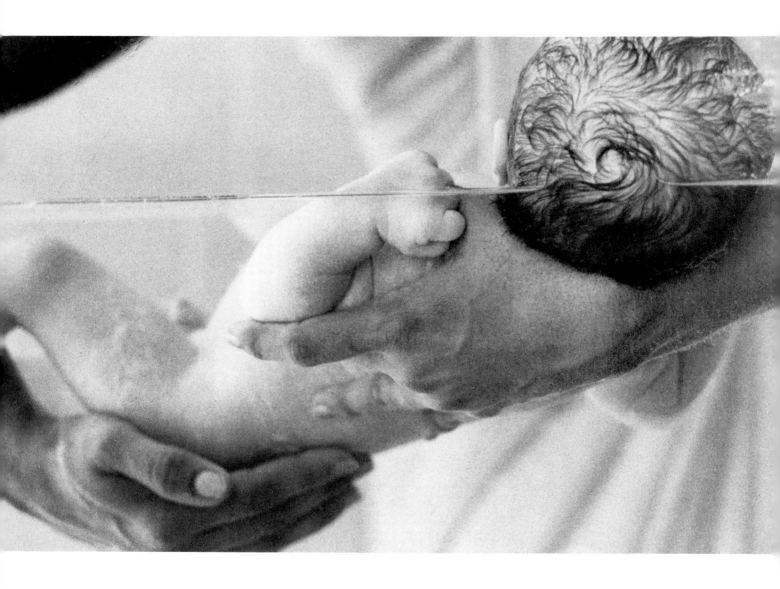

Put your right hand under your baby's sacrum—that is, under the small of the back—or, more likely, the little buttocks will come to rest in the open palm of your right hand.

This double support will give *you* confidence.

And so encourage you to relax.

Which is, of course, the most important thing.

Yes, it is essential that your hands be relaxed.
Otherwise how can your baby feel secure?
Your hands can relax only if your shoulders do, too.
And your shoulders can relax only if you are breathing freely.
Free breathing. We return to it again!
Free breathing, all the time.
Then, and only then, can there be real harmony.
Between both your hands.
Between the child and you.

You see, this little baby is a mirror, as it were,
reflecting your own image back at you.

When you look at your child, you know immediately whether tension is present. Or freedom.

Where?
In the baby?
No!
In you.
Mother, baby;
subject, object;
are they two?
No.
They are one.
One, only one.
As always. As ever.

JUST A FEW MORE POINTS

When is it best to start?

This is a delicate and important point.

In South India, in Kerala, where this art has its origin, it is said that massaging should begin once the baby is one month old.

Now what we have learned from the most recent scientific studies* is that this massaging is performed by all mammals.

They start licking the newborn intensely right after birth.

This appears to be so vital that newborns which have been deprived of this intense licking often die.

Very likely the colics which are so common in infants during the first three months of life will disappear.

Then we must also take into account the disposition of the mother.

Some women are rather shy in touching their babies.

They touch their infants with the tips of their fingers and touch only the extremities, the feet and hands.

They will use the palm of the hand only on the next day.

And fully embrace the infant only after three or four days.

In fact we may assume that these women are highly inhibited.

And therefore we cannot take them as the rule.

Practically speaking I would say: No proper complete massage before the baby is one month old.

No touching of the abdomen, of course, until the umbilical cord is gone.

And in the beginning, very gentle touching rather than actual massaging of the infant's body.

Once the first month is over the real massage begins, and you may apply some pressure.

---

*I would truly recommend that people who are seriously concerned read *Touching* by Ashley Montague. I wish I could quote the whole book from beginning to end. I am greatly indebted to Ashley Montague for providing such valuable information and scientific proofs for so much of what I have been doing and understanding intuitively.

Release the power of life.

But always remember it is not "yours."

It is not "your doing."

You are an instrument through which "it" finds expression.

So you must never be tempted to "use" pressure. That would be adding something of your own.

Never apply pressure.

On the contrary: Relax!

And allow "it" to flow from you.

Look at Shantala's hands.

See how free they are . . .

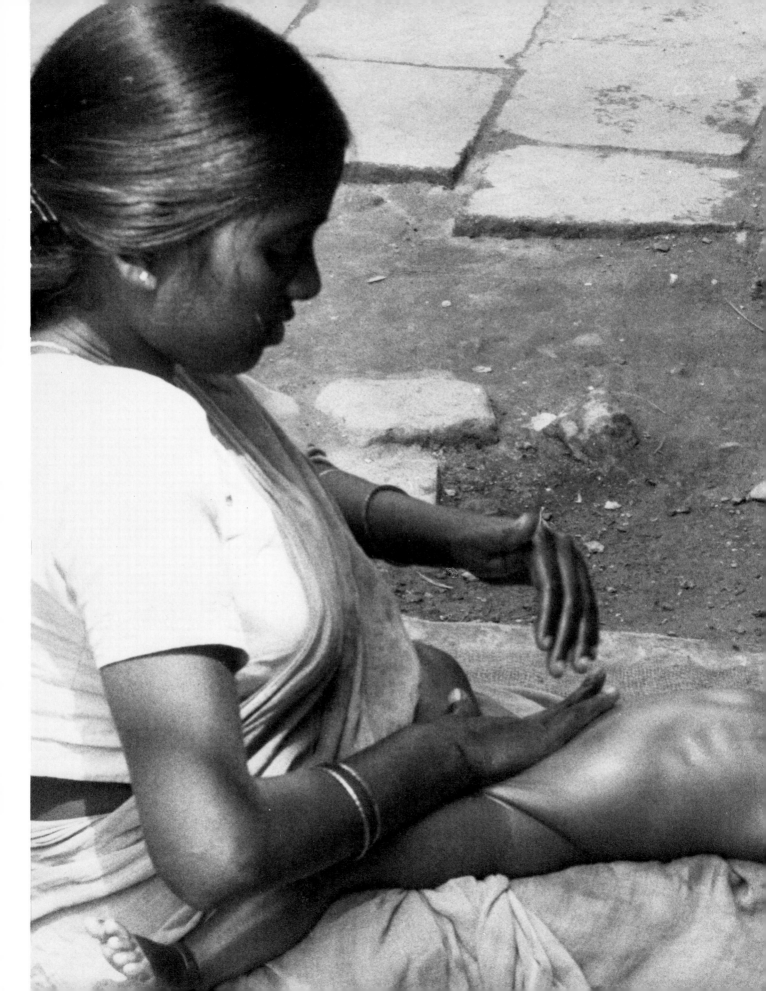

Free . . . relaxed . . .
and yet so full of life
and power . . .

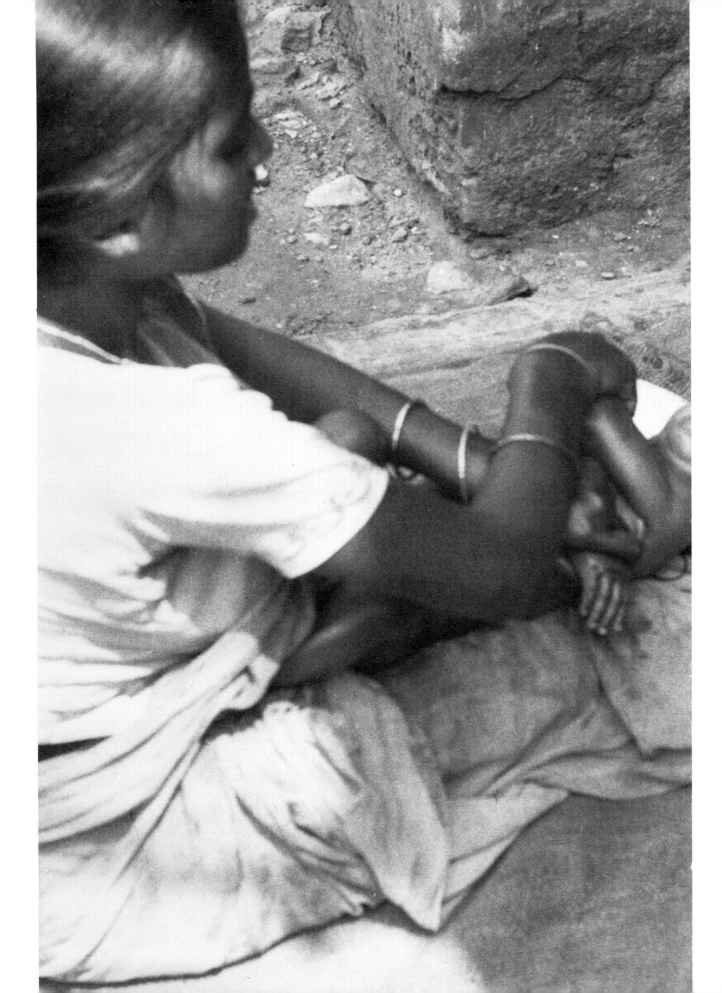

So much power is unleashed . . . !
Isn't it somewhat like a battle?

Couldn't you believe that Shantala
in some fit of madness
is beating her baby
or even trying to kill it!

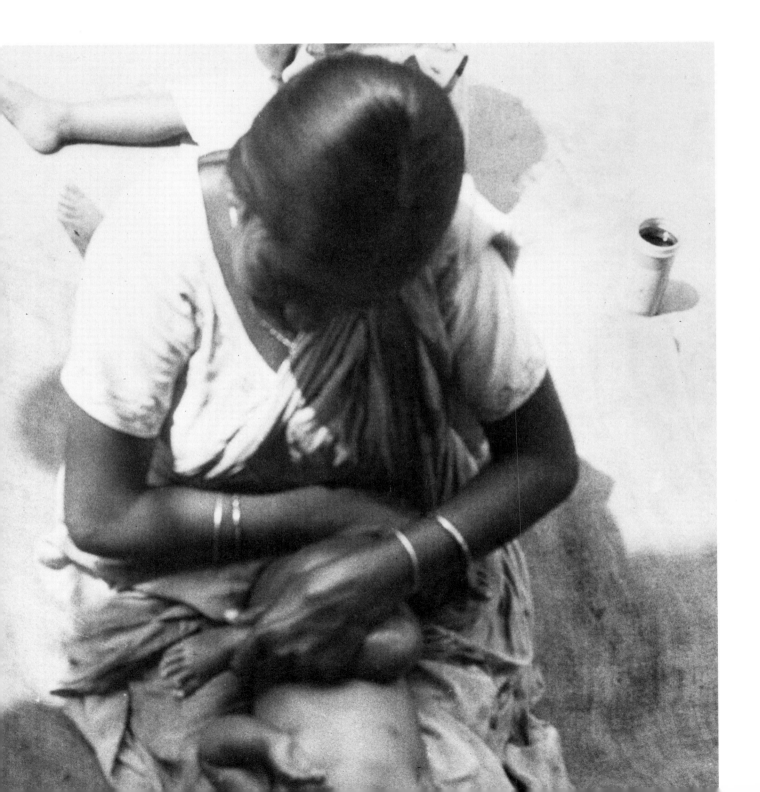

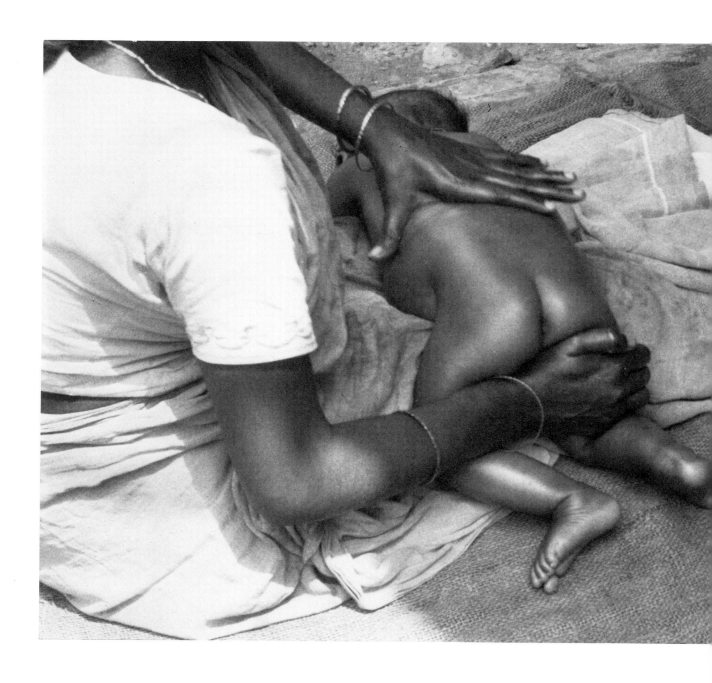

Love and hate can seem too close for comfort, sometimes.
You could almost think that Shantala was spanking the child.
What, then, is the difference?

Spanking can be enjoyed . . .
by the spanker.
While here, obviously, both mother and baby enjoy equally.
What is this mystery?
Here is some kind of fight, no doubt:
the fierce, the sweet battle of love
in which a tremendous flood of energy
is both given and received.

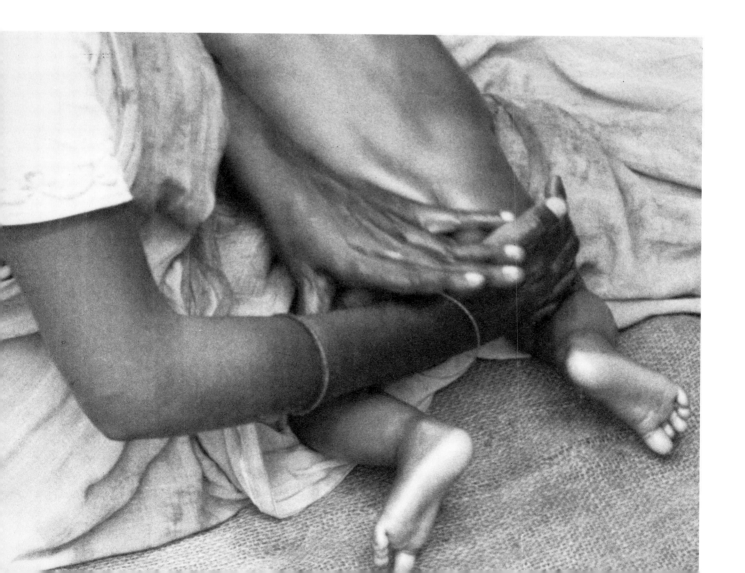

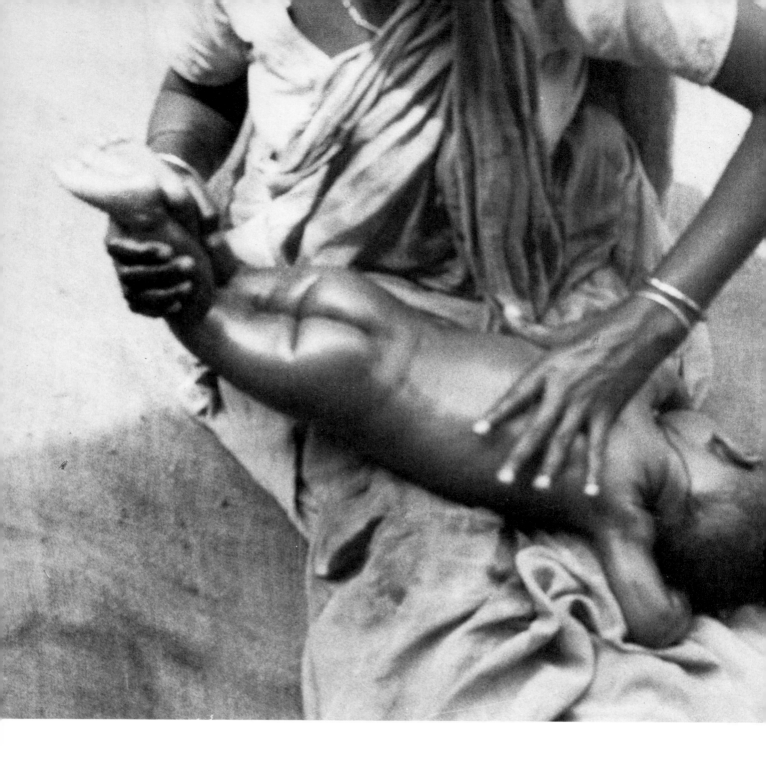

Yes—see, *feel* the tremendous power in Shantala's hands.
And the utter relaxation of the baby.

How long should you keep massaging your baby?
Daily from ten to twenty minutes.
Once or twice a day.

And what is the best time?
Morning, whenever you are free.
And evening just before sleep.

And until what age?
You might say until the baby is from three to six months old.

Or rather until your child can move about and turn over on its stomach all by itself, being able to relax its own back.

Try to remember how it feels in an airplane when you have to remain seated for hours. And how much you want to get up, walk, and stretch.

Yes, just try to realize how the baby's little back must feel.

✥
And yet . . .

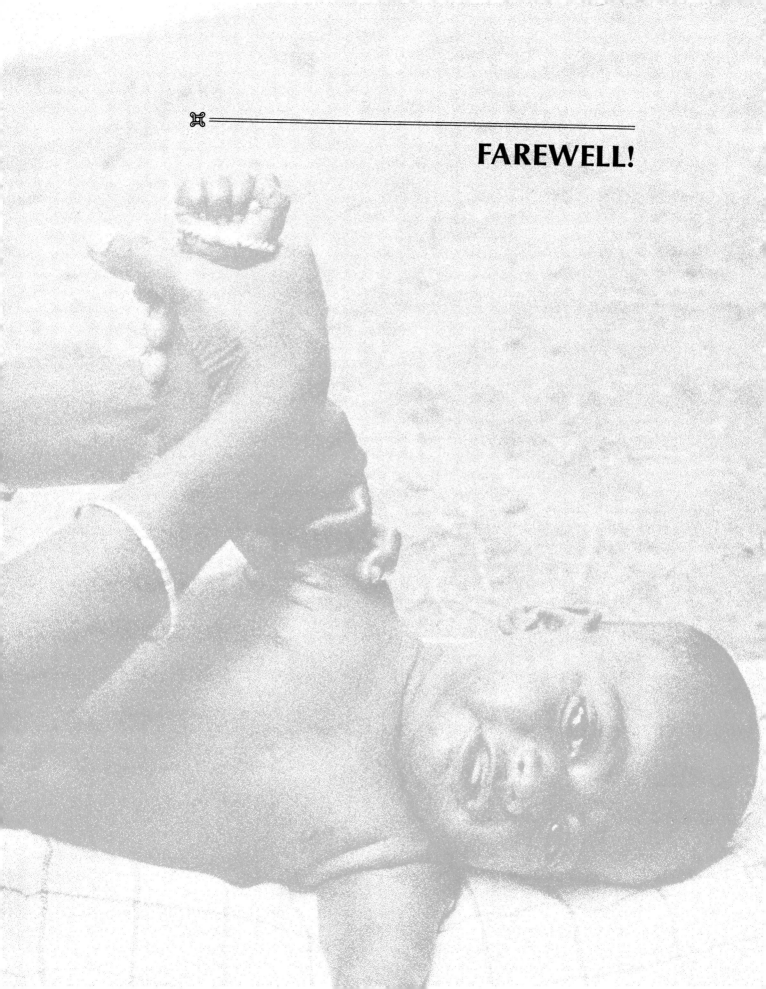

≡

≡

"Until six months!" you may exclaim,
"Half an hour a day!
But I'll never have the time!"
Time . . .
As always, time is the problem.
Or, rather, the mystery.
But do not worry. You will have the time.
And then, as you well know, it takes a lot of time for a tree to grow,
or to raise a child.

≡

In any art, as we have said, there is a technique.
Which one must learn.
Technique and learning take time.
Rather, they *are* in time.
But once this technique is mastered, the artist moves beyond it.
And beyond time.
You touch something in yourself. Or, rather, something starts expressing itself in you.
Something that was there all the time!
Puzzle?
Paradox?
It is the secret, the mystery, of all art.
Art, which enables you to touch the absolute.
With your very human hands!

≡

Whether you will reach this level, or whether you will merely remain a good technician,
is difficult to say.
Is it a question of effort, of persistence?
In a way, yes.
For effort, in the beginning, is necessary.
But then, oddly enough, effort becomes a barrier.
Gracefulness, spontaneity—
can they be learned?

Simple things are . . . so simple.
And yet so difficult!
Sitting on the floor.
Keeping your back straight,
and yet relaxed.
Keeping your shoulders free,
and your neck free as well.
And your legs free, relaxed,
yet straight!
Yes, it is all so simple.
And yet:
"Oh, my poor back! Oh, my legs!"
Simple, indeed, and yet almost impossible!
Impossible for you.
But any child can do it.
Have you watched them?
This is a hard lesson.
But a rich one.
For indeed it touches upon the heart of any true learning.
Learning we confuse most of the time with information.
Information we cram into our heads.
Here you learn with your hands.
With your body.
Indeed with your whole being.

⌘

When you begin with the massaging, your mind keeps wavering.
Going from the book to the baby:
"Ah, yes, I must do it like this . . . and then . . . let me see . . ."
Your mind keeps going from your head to your hands.
From the book to the baby. Then back to your head. Back to the book . . .
And so it oscillates.
Between two.
Two! That would not be too bad.
But, in fact, your mind goes from place to place,
to the chest . . . then to the book . . . then to . . . let me see . . . the arms. Then to the book . . . then to . . . the legs. . . .
Bits and pieces.
That is what you are!

But little by little some kind of continuity will be there. And, quite naturally, your hands will know their way: the chest, the arms, the legs. . . .
Not because it was *in the book*. But owing to some inner necessity.
And then, one day, the book is forgotten completely.
No more oscillating. No more splitting of the mind and hands.
Oneness is not far.

Oneness is not far.
And rhythm soon will carry you from place to place.
Rhythm which is a true necessity.
Massaging, now, is a dance.

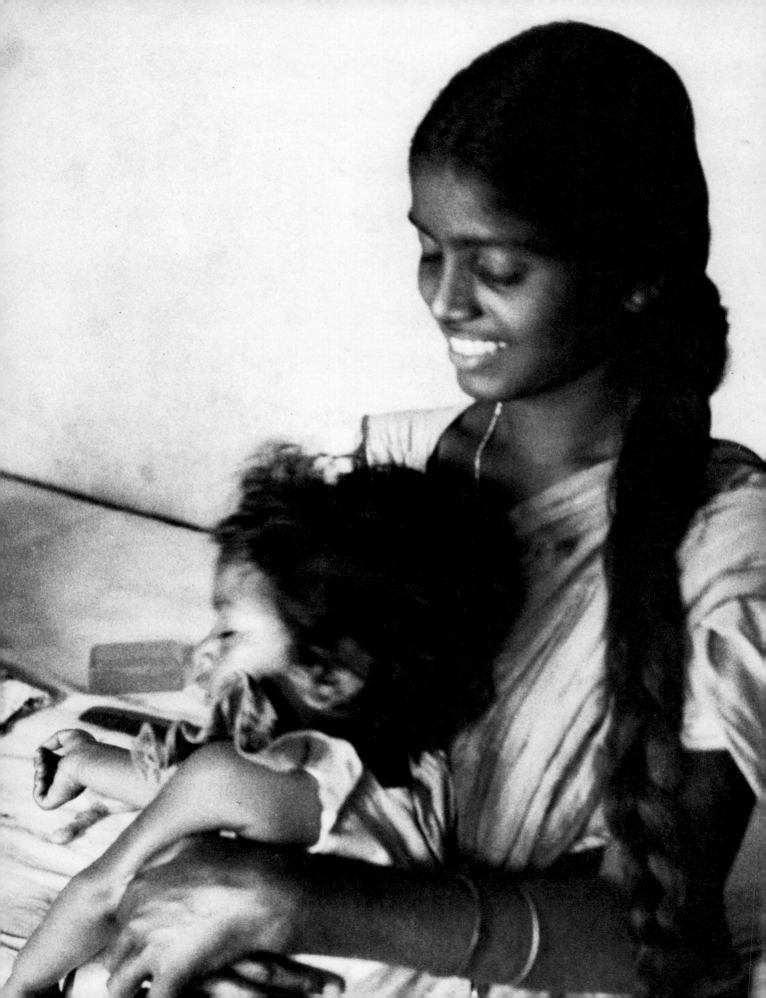

When perfection is reached, where are you?
Where is "you"? And where is "I"?
In perfection how could there be "two"?
Are dancers "two"?
Two and one.
One in two.
And who is it that conducts the dance here?
You?
Is it not rather the child?
It is neither.
Or both.
Rather it is love.
Love which is one
unique breath
breathing in two.

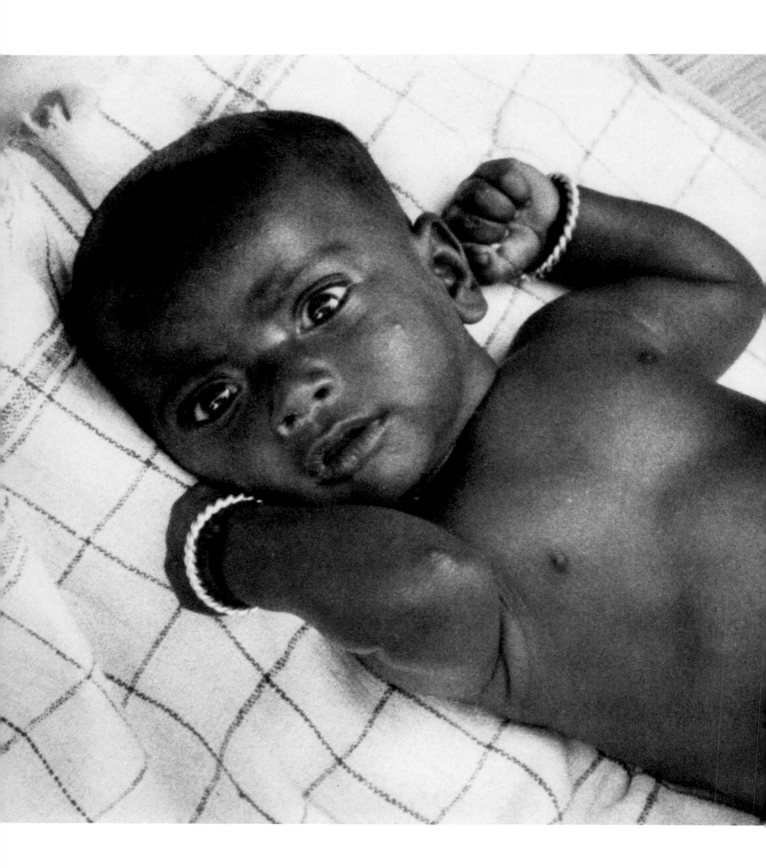

✠

Yes, as you can see, massaging can remain merely a technique, a kind of exercise.

Which, no doubt, will help the child.

Or it may take you far deeper.

Merely a technique. Or an art.

And, for any art, you need a Master.

There are things you simply cannot learn from books.

At this level, books, one might say, are meant for those who know already.

And where are you to find this Master?

Where will you go to learn?

Calcutta?

Where luck put Shantala in my way?

Why not?

She would teach you. Gladly.

But Calcutta is far away. The climate is difficult. And you would have to stay. Things of this kind cannot be learned in one day.

Now you feel lost.

But fortunately you will not have to go that far away.

Everything is nearby. Close at hand. As always.

A Master is here. Waiting for you.

Your baby will teach you!

Your baby will be your Master.

All that is required is attention, openness.

And great simplicity.

⌘

We are in India.

But it is a parable of Chuang Tzü that springs to my mind.

Indeed wisdom knows no frontiers.

He said:

"One day the Duke of Houan was settling down to read in one of the rooms on top of his palace, while down below, Pien, his blacksmith, was making a wheel.

"Putting down his hammer, the blacksmith went up and accosted the Duke:

" 'What are you reading?'

" 'The words of the saints,' replied the Duke.

" 'The saints—are they still alive?'

" 'No,' replied the Duke. 'They are dead.'

" 'Well,' said the blacksmith, 'you're wasting your time. All that you'll find in your book is a lot of old rubbish.'

" 'I am reading,' rejoined the Duke. 'And it is not for a blacksmith to give me his advice! Out of the goodness of my heart I will allow you to explain yourself. Otherwise you would be sentenced to death for your lack of respect.'

" 'Very well,' said the blacksmith. 'This is what work has taught your humble servant.

" 'When I am making a wheel and I take it slowly, work is pleasant. But the results are not sound.

" 'When I go fast, the work is a strain. And the results are slapdash.

" 'One must go neither too slow nor too fast. There is a rhythm one must find that suits the hand, but springs from the heart.

" 'There is something here that is simply too deep for words. Something I've never been able to make my own son understand. And which, unfortunately, he has never succeeded in learning for himself.

" 'And so here I am, despite my seventy years of age, still making wheels.' "

The wisdom that the Ancients have not been able to pass on in ways other than words is truly dead.

And it's nothing but the residue you will find in your books.

AND WHO IS SHANTALA?

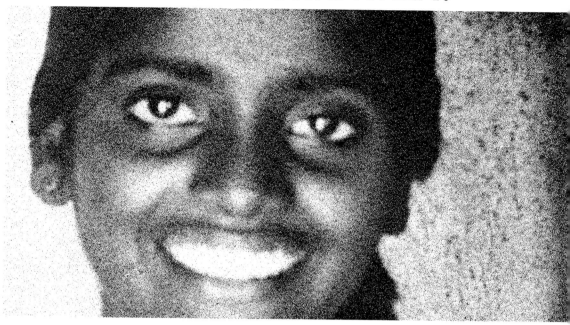

It was in Calcutta that I met Shantala.

And certainly it was my good fortune which took me there.

Calcutta! The city which makes Westerners tremble with horror and indignation.

Calcutta, where an insane surfeit of population is piled up, attracted by the mirage of the big city, all fleeing the thousand and one calamities which are, in India more than anywhere else, the very warp of life.

Yes, there was Shantala, in Pilkana, the poorest—I was about to write, the most sordid—of all the shantytowns that have cropped up in this most wretched and outcast of all Indian cities.

A charitable organization, Seva Sangha Samiti, had founded right there a hostel where, in the midst of utter poverty, the most destitute could find help, patient understanding, and friendliness.

Shantala was living there, helping with children.

And there she was outside the hostel, one beautiful sunny morning, massaging her baby.

I stopped short, struck by what I was witnessing: In the midst of filth and misery, a spectacle of purest beauty.

A silent dialogue of love between a mother and her baby.

Some kind of ritual or ballet—slowness, controlled strength, tenderness, and dignity.

All the hideous aspects of the place and of the streets I had passed through suddenly disappeared.

Nothing existed any longer but the light, and that love.

What a lesson!

Suddenly I could understand why Job on his dunghill would not complain. "Who are you to judge Me?"

A saying they have in India came singing into my mind:

"It is in the mud that the lotus flower has its root.

"From mud it grows,

"and through filthy waters

"drawn irresistibly

"by a light it does not yet even know.

"It is love, it is light

"that guides and forces

"the flower

"in its difficult path upward.

"Light that will flood it suddenly

"once, the surface being reached,

"it breaks through

"and blossoms open fully."

I remained there silent and confused.

I felt almost like an intruder, witnessing by accident such an exchange of love.

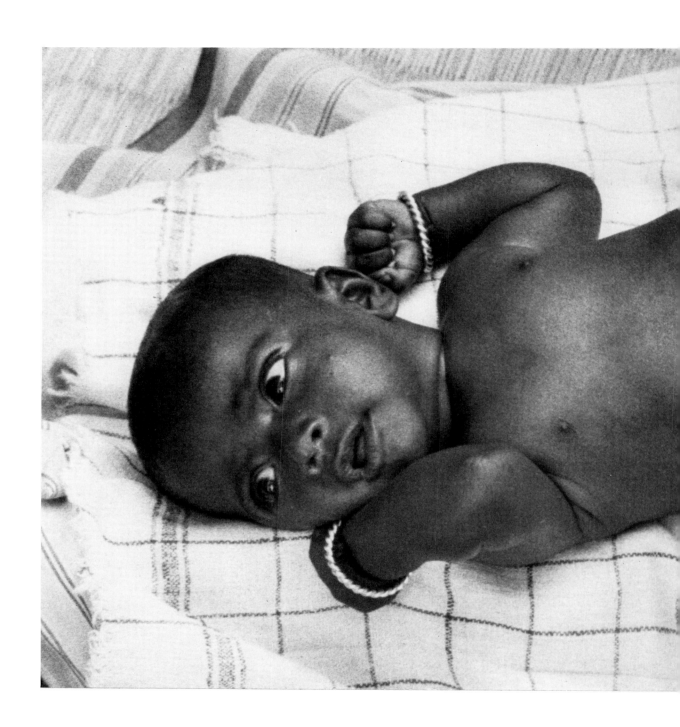

When it was over and Shantala realized I was there, I asked her permission to come the following day and take photographs.

Out of simplicity and affection (I had previously been able to help her in some way) she agreed.

I came the next day.

In fact I came day after day.

For indeed there was so much to learn.

Shantala taught me.

And so did her baby.

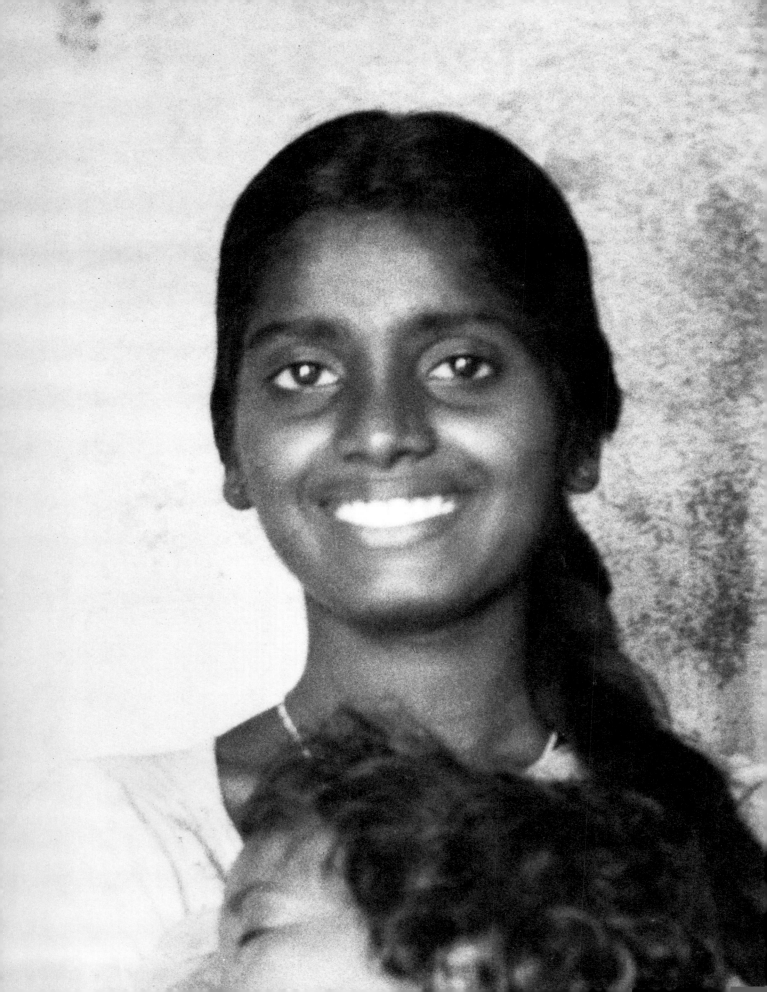

I took the photographs like a painter, trying to capture the elusive secret of beauty.

And there it was.

Love and light,

and life and its pulsation.

And silence and dignity.

ACKNOWLEDGMENTS

I cannot end this story without mentioning Leo and Françoise Jalais, since it is through them that I met Shantala.

I wish to express not only my gratitude but also my admiration for these wonderful people and their work of love and charity.

Very close to Mother Teresa, living for the poor with the poor, they started working for Brothers to All Men and work now for Seva Sangha Samiti, a very similar charitable organization more specifically concerned with India.

Anyone who would like to learn from Shantala may get in touch with her through these friends, whose address I give here:

"SEVA SANGHA SAMITI"

5 BL ROY ROAD

PILKANA . HOWRAH

WEST BENGAL, INDIA

A NOTE ABOUT THE TYPE

The text of this book was set in linotype Optima, a typeface
designed by Hermann Zapf from 1952–55 and issued in 1958.
In designing Optima, Zapf created a truly new type form—
a cross between the classic roman and a sans-serif face.
So delicate are the stresses and balances in Optima that it rivals
sans-serif faces in clarity and freshness and old-style faces in
variety and interest.

The book was composed by Dix Typesetting Company Inc.,
Syracuse, New York.
Typography, binding and jacket design by Helen Barrow.
Printed by Halliday Lithograph, West Hanover, Massachusetts.